CHINA OR JAPAN
WHICH WILL LEAD ASIA?

The series in Comparative Politics and International Studies

Series editor, Christophe Jaffrelot

This series consists of translations of noteworthy manuscripts and publications in the social sciences emanating from the foremost French researchers at Sciences Po, Paris.

The focus of the series is the transformation of politics and society by transnational and domestic factors—globalisation, migration and the post-bipolar balance of power on the one hand, and ethnicity and religion on the other. States are more permeable to external influence than ever before and this phenomenon is accelerating processes of social and political change the world over. In seeking to understand and interpret these transformations, this series gives priority to social trends from below as much as to the interventions of state and non-state actors.

CLAUDE MEYER

CHINA OR JAPAN

Which Will Lead Asia?

Translated by
Adrian Shaw

HURST & COMPANY, LONDON

First published in 2010 as *Chine ou Japon,*
quel leader pour l'Asie? by Presses de Sciences Po
© 2010 Presses de Sciences po

This English translation
first published in the United Kingdom in 2011 by
C. Hurst & Co. (Publishers) Ltd.,
41 Great Russell Street, London, WC1B 3PL
© C. Hurst & Co. (Publishers) Ltd., 2011
Translation © Adrian Shaw, 2011
All rights reserved.
Printed in India

The right of Claude Meyer to be identified as the author
of this publication is asserted by him in accordance with
the Copyright, Designs and Patents Act, 1988.

A Cataloguing-in-Publication data record for this book
is available from the British Library.

ISBN: 978-1-84904-172-0 *hardback*
       978-1-84904-215-4 *paperback*

This book is printed on paper from registered sustainable
and managed sources.

www.hurstpub.co.uk

For Tania

CONTENTS

CONTENTS

CONTENTS

PREFACE

Since 11 March 2011, Japan has been facing what prime minister Naoto Kan has called its biggest crisis since the Second World War. The earthquake, with a magnitude of nine on the Richter scale, which struck off Japan's north-east coast on that day was the most powerful in the country's history, stronger than the Kobe quake in 1995 or even that which destroyed almost the whole of Tokyo in 1923. It was followed by a massive tsunami, with some waves reaching a height of 77 feet and in some cases travelling up to nine miles inland. In addition to the enormous damage in the three prefectures hit by both events, the tsunami knocked out several reactors at the Fukushima nuclear power station. In doing so it triggered the world's biggest nuclear crisis since Chernobyl in 1986, as fears increased of an uncontrollable meltdown of the nuclear fuel if the damaged cooling functions could not be restored.

The human tragedy is clearly the most terrible consequence of these three combined disasters. According to provisional casualty reports released by the Japanese authorities, almost 11,000 people have died, 17,000 have been declared missing and more than 240,000 are homeless. The toll may also be heavy among the technicians working to restore cooling systems at the nuclear plant. The number of victims and the lifetime consequences for their health will vary dramatically depending on the success or failure of this process and the length of their exposure to high levels of radiation.

The economic consequences will also be very serious, not only in the devastated prefectures but in the country as a whole, because Japanese industry functions on the "zero stock" model. Factories, especially in the crucial electronics and automobile sectors, had to be closed in many parts of the country as they were lacking components manufactured in the north-east. Not stopping at Japan's borders, the shockwave will be felt throughout the whole of Asia's "integrated circuit" described in this book. Its geographical centre may be situated in China, where most assembly takes place, but its technological nerve centre is in Japan.

The economic impact will be twofold, through the cost of reconstruction and a decline in output. The cost of reconstruction could be double that of the Kobe earthquake: in the most pessimistic scenario, the Japanese authorities have not ruled out a figure of USD 310 billion, close to 6 per cent of GDP. In the economy, a recession is likely during the second and third quarter of 2011 but will be followed by a strong rebound during the reconstruction period. All in all, economic growth could be nil or slightly negative in 2011, then resume in 2012. These estimates are made at the date of this preface and do not take into account any dramatic deterioration of the situation at the Fukushima nuclear plant, which is quite possible given the alarming news released by the operator and the government. In all events, the nuclear accident will have far-reaching consequences for Japan's energy sources, as the closure of the Fukushima plant—and probably several others in similar locations and with the same safety standards—will impose a reassessment of the energy policies in place since the 1970s. Japan will have to import more fossil fuels, especially liquid natural gas, which will weigh on its energy bill and further increase its dependency on other countries for its energy mix.

That being said, Japan as the world's third-largest economy and leading creditor has the means to finance the immediate reconstruction costs, which represent only 3 per cent of its public debt and 1.5 per cent of national wealth. True, Japan's public debt is high, but it is 95 per cent financed by Japanese residents. There is little dependence on foreign investors and the country's gross saving rate remains comfortable. Japan also has vast liquid assets abroad, some of which could be repatriated, provided that it was done gradually so as not to disrupt the markets.

More broadly, economic growth is founded on confidence in the future. The psychological effect of the disaster on the Japanese population will have indirect effects on prospects for growth. Beyond the structural handicaps for robust growth, such as a declining population, public debt and a lack of political leadership, probably of greater concern is the loss of Japan's confidence in its own future, evident in deflation, a falling birth rate and a form of isolationism. The 1990 crisis was as much moral as economic and it has stripped Japan of the strong national will that once forced it to excel. Since then, a disenchanted country seems to have been moving backwards into the future. But maybe there will be a "before" and an "after Fukushima." Already a truce, if not a sacred union, has been established at a political level. The Emperor, symbol of the nation, expressed his compassion for the victims on television, the only imperial declaration since his father Hirohito's historic radio announcement of Japan's surrender in 1945. Hopefully, the stoicism and solidarity shown by the people in their present troubles will translate into a national revival that could stir up the country to regain control of its own destiny in a defiant response to this triple disaster.

That is my sincerest hope for a country with which I have developed such close links over many years. To my Japanese friends and to Japanese readers of this book I express my deepest sympathy and my admiration for the stoicism and dignity you have shown over the past few weeks.

Claude Meyer
30 March 2011

FOREWORD

Readers can let their own interests or priorities guide them in this book. The first part (Chapters 1 and 2) is predominantly economic: it looks at the respective paths taken by China and Japan and how those paths have crossed in history, the strengths and weaknesses of their economies, the impact of the global crisis and the challenges they face in the future.

The second part (Chapters 3 and 4) considers the rival ambitions of China and Japan in the quest for supremacy in Asia, with the dialectical relationship between economic and strategic power serving as a guiding thread. In China's case, the priority is to accelerate the process of catching up in the economic sphere in order to consolidate its strategic influence as a regional leader and global power. For Japan, it is to safeguard its economic leadership through technological supremacy while at the same time "normalising" its strategic positioning in Asia and the world to make it commensurate with its economic and financial weight.

The conclusion outlines the most likely scenario for this stand-off between China and Japan.

ACKNOWLEDGEMENTS

I would like to thank everyone who has helped me over the last few years with the publication of this book, originally in French and subsequently in English and other languages.

I owe a particular debt of thanks to those who read the French manuscript and enriched it with their feedback. I am profoundly grateful to Christian Sautter, whose teaching helped me to develop a taste for economic research: as with a previous work for which he wrote a preface, this book owes much to his detailed comments, some of which encouraged me to open up the outlook for the future in Asia. Thanks to Jean Luc Domenach for his immediate support for a still-vague project, and for his precious observations on some key points; thanks also to Michel de Grandi for his willingness to share his vast knowledge of China and Japan with me. I am, of course, solely responsible for any shortcomings and for the opinions expressed in this book.

My thanks go to all the staff at Presses de Sciences Po, especially Executive Director Marie-Geneviève Vandesande for accepting the project and Series Director Alain Dieckhoff for his benign and rigorous oversight.

I thank Patrick Messerlin for inviting me to join the Groupe d'Economie Mondiale (GEM) research centre at Sciences Po and the Sciences Po Masters department for asking me to teach the courses which provide the framework for this book. My thanks also go to the International Department of Sciences Po,

ACKNOWLEDGEMENTS

the Asia Pacific Centre team and its director Alessia Lefébure, Jean-Marie Bouissou, David Camroux and Christophe Jaffrelot of the Centre for International Studies and Research (CERI), Jean-François Sabouret, head of the Asia Network, and all the students whose essays and discussions have stimulated my thinking over the years.

I extend my thanks to colleagues in China, South Korea, Japan and the United States who have welcomed me on teaching or research visits, enabling me to gain greater insights into some of the matters raised in this book. I am particularly grateful to my friends at Columbia University—Gerald Curtis, Xiaobo Lu and Hugh Patrick—at Keio University—Naoyuki Yoshino and Sahoko Kaji—and at the Chinese University of Hong Kong.

I would also like to thank Institut CDC pour la Recherche and its Scientific Director Isabelle Laudier for their support for publication.

For the English version, I should first thank C. Hurst & Co. (Publishers), London and Columbia University Press, New York, who co-publish this book. My personal thanks for their dedication to this project go to the editor Michael Dwyer and to Daisy Leitch of C. Hurst & Co. (Publishers), as well as to Christophe Jaffrelot, the series editor, and Irina Vauday at CERI-Sciences Po. I am very grateful to the translator Adrian Shaw for the excellent cooperation we developed during the translation process and to David Goodwin, who read the English manuscript and made very useful comments.

Last but not least, thanks to Dyssia for her support and patience.

ABBREVIATIONS AND CONVENTIONS

ADB	Asian Development Bank
APAC	Asia Pacific, including East Asia, the Indian sub-continent, Australasia (Australia and New Zealand) and Oceania
APEC	Asia Pacific Economic Cooperation, a forum of twenty-one Asian and Western countries on the Pacific Rim, including the United States, Russia, Japan and China
APT	ASEAN Plus Three
ASEAN	Association of South-East Asian Nations (Brunei, Cambodia, Indonesia, Laos, Malaysia, Myanmar, the Philippines, Singapore, Thailand and Vietnam)
ASEAN+3	ASEAN Plus Three, or APT (ASEAN countries plus China, South Korea and Japan)
ASEAN+6	ASEAN+3 plus Australia, India and New Zealand
BRIC	Brazil, Russia, India, China
CMI	Chiang Mai Initiative
CMIM	Chiang Mai Initiative Multilateralisation
CPC	Communist Party of China
CSA	Currency Swap Arrangement
DPJ	Democratic Party of Japan
EAC	East Asian Community (project)

ABBREVIATIONS AND CONVENTIONS

EAS	East Asia Summit, between the members of ASEAN+6
FDI	Foreign Direct Investment
FTA	Free-Trade Agreement
GDP	Gross Domestic Product
IEA	International Energy Agency
JETRO	Japan External Trade Organisation
LDP	Liberal Democratic Party
MITI	Ministry of International Trade and Industry, replaced in 2001 by METI, Ministry of Economy, Trade and Industry
NAFTA	North American Free-Trade Agreement
NIAC 1	Newly Industrialised Asian Countries 1: South Korea, Hong Kong, Singapore and Taiwan (the "Dragons")
NIAC 2	Newly Industrialised Asian Countries 2: Malaysia, Thailand, Indonesia, the Philippines and Brunei (the "Tigers")
ODA	Official Development Assistance
PRC	People's Republic of China
SCO	Shanghai Cooperation Organisation (China, Russia, Kazakhstan, Kyrgyzstan, Tajikistan and Uzbekistan)
SDF	Self-Defence Forces (Japan)
UN	United Nations
UNCTAD	United Nations Conference on Trade and Development

East Asia comprises China, Japan, South Korea, Hong Kong, Taiwan and the ten ASEAN countries.

Except where otherwise stated, GDP is expressed in US dollars at market exchange rates, not purchasing power parities (which take account of differences in purchasing power between national currencies).

ABBREVIATIONS AND CONVENTIONS

Statistics for China and Japan are taken from annual editions of *China Statistical Yearbook* and *Japan Statistical Yearbook* except where otherwise stated.

In accordance with the custom in English, Japanese names are written with the given name followed by the family name (e.g. Yukio Hatoyama) and Chinese names with the family name followed by the given name (e.g. Deng Xiaoping).

INTRODUCTION

The Tokyo Olympics in 1964 and the Osaka Universal Exposition in 1970 symbolised the renaissance of Japan, which in 1968 became the "third great power" after the USA and the Soviet Union.[1] Forty years later, following a similar pattern, the Beijing Olympics in 2008 and the Shanghai World Expo 2010 have crowned China's spectacular return to the international stage. And spectacular is indeed the word to describe China's rise, ousting Japan as the world's second-largest economy, having eased Germany out of third place just three years earlier.

The Shanghai World Expo 2010, twenty times bigger than the 2008 event in Zaragoza, gives the measure of the remarkable transformation that the city known as the Pearl of the East has experienced over the last thirty years, and the whole of China with it. From the 100th floor of the World Financial Center one's gaze is drawn to the forest of skyscrapers that marks Pudong, a showcase for Chinese modernity which has sprung from nowhere in under fifteen years. To the south, the eye takes in the site of the World Expo complex, the first in a developing country, then to the west the Bund and the majestic architecture of People's Square. To the south-west, it may dwell on the concession granted to France in 1849, the St. Ignatius Cathedral; in nearby Guangxi Park lies "Paul" Xu Guangxi, the celebrated scholar baptised by the Jesuit Matteo Ricci in 1603. In a single sweep, the vista thus embraces three defining moments in Chi-

1

na's encounter with the West: the cultural and scientific dialogue with the Jesuits, the humiliating period of concessions and the World Expo, which finally marks China's return to its rightful place as a world power.

The curious visitor will learn that the technological achievements embodied in this 492-metre tower are the work of the Japanese developer and architect Mori, and the optimist will be tempted to see in this the seeds of a promising cooperation between China and Japan, the dominant powers of Asia. And yet, most unusually in international relations, their political relations have deteriorated profoundly since the turn of the century, while conversely their trade links have been growing at breakneck speed. The revival of nationalist sentiment and memories of unhealed wounds partly explain these acute tensions, but their deeper cause lies elsewhere.

The world's second and third-largest economic powers may be locked in step but their rivalry and mutual mistrust springs from an identical ambition, namely to become the dominant force in Asia, to which the global economy's centre of gravity is inexorably being drawn. That transfer of economic power is already well under way. The nineteenth century was Europe's, the twentieth America's and the twenty-first will doubtless be Asia's or, more accurately, of Asia's return to the pre-eminent position in the global economy that it occupied before its eclipse in the nineteenth century.[2] The Asia-Pacific region now accounts for 25 per cent of global output compared with 12 per cent in 1970 and the percentage is likely to rise to 35 per cent by 2020, and even 50 per cent by 2050, as the hundreds of millions of people joining the middle classes drive the rapid expansion of domestic markets. In financial terms, over 60 per cent of international reserves are held by Asian countries, China and Japan being the foremost among them.

And yet Asia has not been immune to the turmoil that struck the global economy in 2008–2009. Given the severity and the systemic nature of the crisis, coupled with Asia's growing influence, there is a pressing need to take a close look at the profound shifts taking place in the region, especially a process of integration that could lead to the creation of an economic community. According to a widely held view, Asia's future is already mapped out, between the ineluctable decline of Japan on the one hand and the irresistible rise of China and India on the other. But such a simplistic view is probably ill-advised, just as the notion of an unstoppable Japan proved to be, since it fails to take into account the still relatively small economic importance of India, Japan's economic and financial domination of Asia and the uncertainty of long-term forecasts.

Let us look at the first of those factors: the economic weight of India and, more broadly, the relevance of the "Chindia" concept. The term, coined by an Indian politician, has been adopted by the international media when referring to the simultaneous emergence of China and India as a source of upheaval for the established global order. The argument is that these two Asian giants, which represent a third of the world's population and have complementary advantages, will soon impose themselves as dominant economic powers in Asia and then globally. But that is to forget that India is only the world's twelfth-largest economy, with GDP less than a third the size of China's, and that its growth rate is still significantly lower, averaging 7.6 per cent between 2001 and 2010 compared with China's 9.5 per cent. Although appealing, the "Chindia" concept tends merely to muddy the waters if employed without specifying when the predicted upheaval will occur.

Japan's resilience is the second criterion to take into consideration, contrary to the image—misleading although magnified by the crisis—of an enfeebled country sliding inexorably into a foretold decline. The global recession has hit Japan very hard, compounding in a sort of double whammy the profound internal crisis it endured in the 1990s. And yet the country emerged stronger from that first long slump, for the decade was not "lost." Reforms put off for too long enabled Japan to renew itself and find a better fit with ongoing globalisation, of which it had previously tended to be on the receiving end. Will the same be true of the current crisis? No-one knows, for the change of governing party in September 2009—the first real alternation of power in post-war Japan—has ushered in a period of great uncertainty. But the country still has much going for it and any analysis of the future balance of power in Asia must take full account of that, without surrendering to a "declinism" that all too often sets an anaemic, ageing Japan against a rampant, dynamic China.

The third factor is the uncertain nature of long-term forecasts, except where demographics are concerned. On that point we should bear in mind that Japan is a greying nation and that China will follow suit from 2015; their ageing populations will weigh on growth throughout the region, for between them the two countries account for 77 per cent of East Asia's GDP. While demographic projections are relatively reliable, long-term economic forecasts are less so because by definition they cannot include essential qualitative factors such as social unrest, political instability, financial crisis, etc. When Japan was at the peak of its power in 1989, few observers would have dared predict the stagnation in which the country was mired throughout the 1990s. All the more reason, then, for the current global crisis to make us suspicious of long-term forecasts, given the extent to which regulators and economists, with a few rare exceptions, were caught wrong-footed. Moreover, we have not yet seen the full effect of that profound shock to the system. Uncertainty lingers over possible aftershocks and the global economy is most likely heading for a long period of instability.

Given that long-term economic projections are so unreliable, especially those that extend beyond a twenty-year horizon, we shall concentrate here on the period from 2010 to 2030. It may be a debatable choice: this book will not have much to say about India because between now and 2025 its economic influence will still be small in relation to its strategic importance in the region. Likewise, the role of the United States may seem somewhat underplayed for a key actor on the Asian stage. But its place in Asia was more akin to that of a power behind the throne until President Obama undertook his eight-day tour of East Asia in November 2009. Portraying himself as the first Pacific-American president, having spent part of his childhood in Hawaii and Indonesia, he clearly indicated that the trans-Pacific relationship was central to his strategic thinking. American influence is endemic in a region whose socio-political order it substantially shaped and where it still exercises powerful strategic control through a strong military presence and a complex web of alliances. Influence is also brought to bear through the massive power of American multinationals and banks in the region. And we should not forget the dollar's role as a reserve currency and the monetary standard for many Asian countries, or the soft power represented by the pull of American culture and American universities. The US is never very far away in the face-off between China and Japan, and those complex triangular relations will be considered. However, the narrower field of bilateral relations between China and Japan will remain our principal focus here, because they are crucial to the redrawing of the new landscape taking shape in East Asia. The upheavals of the next twenty years can even now be seen in outline: the future of Asia and the broader geopolitical realignments yet to come will depend to a considerable extent on the outcome of the struggle between the world's second and third-largest economies for pre-eminence in Asia, not only in economic but also in political and strategic terms.

This book aims to identify the key features of that battle for supremacy in Asia and thereby to inform the debate about the future shape of the world. It is each protagonist's ambition to become a global power; coming out on top in Asia is a necessary step on the way. Without neglecting the political and strategic aspects, priority will be given to an economic approach because that is the primary arena in which Asian integration is taking place. It is also the one in which China aims to topple Japan, through both the speed with which its economy is catching up and the central place it occupies in global trade and manufacturing.

A meteoric rise for China, a rocky road for Japan: after a brief survey of their diverging paths over the last thirty years or so, we will consider the two rivals' strengths and weaknesses and the major challenges both will face over the next two decades. The second part of the book will look at the key issue of leadership in Asia, which assumes both the desire and the legitimacy to take on that role, not only in economic but also in political and strategic terms. In evaluating those parameters we will be guided by the dialectical relationship between economics and strategic power.[3] Paul Kennedy has undertaken a long-period analysis of the relationship between wealth and power in *The Rise and Fall of the Great Powers*, stating the nature of his enquiry in the introduction: "What this book concentrates upon is the interaction between economics and strategy as each of the leading states in the international system strove to enhance its wealth and its power to become or to remain both rich and strong."[4]

To become a "prosperous and powerful" nation (*fuqiang*) is indeed China's current aim, as it was in the Meiji restoration of 1868, which enabled Japan to impose itself as a regional and global force. Now, the region's two dominant countries are on opposite sides of the wealth-power dialectic. Japan is undisputedly Asia's leading economy but its pacifist constitution deprives it of certain strategic options available to China. Conversely, China is seeking to close the economic gap in double-quick time and ultimately to impose itself as the region's only global power, capable of projecting its supremacy in both the economic and the strategic sphere. China's pursuit of power, masked by the "peaceful rise" mantra, is matched by Japan's aspiration to a "normalisation" that would enable it to vigorously assert itself in strategic matters on the regional and global stage.

"Peaceful rise" for China, desire for "normalisation" for Japan: whatever the catchphrase, what are the implications of this power quest for the future economic and strategic configuration of Asia? Economic partners by force of circumstance but still strategic rivals, China and Japan are kept at odds not only by a burdensome past but also, and above all, by their conflicting ambitions. For the time being, neither of these two dominant powers can lay claim to overall supremacy in the region; is it illusory or premature to imagine that leadership might be shared in a genuine partnership that would greatly contribute to the prosperity and stability of the whole region?

In all events, Europeans should not stand above the debate about Asia's future lest they find themselves sidelined when the cards in the global game are redistributed. By 2030 Asia will be home to three of the world's four mightiest economies. The formation of an Asian Community along European lines is the main thrust of the new Japanese government's foreign policy. The future Asia maps out for itself through regional integration will also be ours, since the destiny of Europe, and of its industries and universities, is also being shaped in Tokyo and Beijing.

1

GENEALOGIES OF TWO ECONOMIC GIANTS

China's meteoric rise is without historical precedent. In a mere thirty years this vast country of 1.3 billion people has pulled itself out of under-development to become the world's second-largest economy,[1] destabilising the international equilibrium and reordering the established hierarchy of the great economic powers. Today, China's GDP accounts for 8 per cent of global output and is already larger than Japan's, whereas it was only a quarter the size just ten years ago. Since 1981, domestic output has grown by a factor of twelve and income per capita by a factor of nine. The proportion of the population living below the poverty line (the equivalent of one US dollar a day) has fallen from 63 to 9 per cent, whereas in sub-Saharan Africa it has remained more or less unchanged at around 40 per cent over the same period.[2] In the developed world, however, China's success elicits more concern than admiration: it became the world's biggest exporter in 2009 with a market share of 9 per cent, compared with only 1 per cent in 1980, and Chinese dominance in certain sectors threatens whole swathes of industry across Europe and the United States.

Without playing down these impressive achievements, they need to be seen in perspective, from both a historical and a geographical standpoint. First let us take the historical context. In 1735, the Jesuit priest Jean-Baptiste du Halde noted that trade within China was incomparably greater than that of all Europe.[3] Adam Smith came to the same conclusion in 1776, finding China "a country much richer than any part of Europe."[4] The leading economic power for centuries, China still represented over 30 per cent of world GDP in 1820 compared with 23 per cent for Europe and only 3 per cent for Japan.[5] However, the historical tide turned against China and there followed a lengthy period of decline. Since 1978, China has enjoyed a new golden age that is merely the first stage of a renaissance fully in keeping with its size, natural resources and human capital. From a geographical perspective, while sheer size and the length of the growth cycle make China's achievements look exceptional, they are comparable to those of other neighbouring countries that have experienced similar growth rates: the Little Dragons,[6] then the Tigers,[7] but most of all Japan. There are many similarities between China's industrial revolution from 1978 to 2008 and Japan's two-stage industrialisation, first following the Meiji "revolution" in 1868, then during the decades of reconstruction and expansion after the country's defeat in 1945.

Japan likewise achieved 10 per cent average annual growth between 1955 and 1973, a period brought to an abrupt end by the oil and financial shocks of the 1970s. Shaken, Japan emerged battle-hardened and stronger, wielding apparently invincible economic and financial might throughout the 1980s, only to become mired in stagnation in the following decade. Its recovery since 2002 owes much to China's expansion. Each of these two great Asian powers has evolved in its own particular way, though their destinies are linked in a seesaw movement of emulation and rivalry. Against the spectacular awakening of China is set Japan's resilience throughout the cycles of crisis and recovery.

China's awakening

After more than a century of economic decline, political instability, war and humiliation, China took formal control of its own destiny with the proclamation in 1949 of the People's Republic. Allied with the USSR, Beijing relied on the technical and financial support provided by its mentor to promote an economic revival based on the collectivisation of agriculture and the development of heavy industry by state-owned companies. Annual growth between 1949 and 1978 amounted to around 5 per cent, the same as the global average, but income per capita rose only slowly due to a population explosion. Great strides were made in healthcare[8] and education, but China in 1978 was still a very poor country with a mainly agrarian economy. Its people had recently suffered two traumatic events: the failure of the Great Leap Forward (1958–61), followed by a terrible famine that caused millions of deaths, then the Cultural Revolution (1966–76),[9] which plunged the education system into chaos,[10] destroyed administrative structures and drained the nation's lifeblood.

The break with the past made by Deng Xiaoping in 1978 was rooted in paradox.[11] His reform policy, the springboard for exceptional economic growth, was not the fruit of an ambitious, preconceived plan but the pragmatic response to an essentially political concern, since the very legitimacy of the Party's control over the state was at stake. Within China, famine, anarchy and power struggles threatened the regime's stability. Abroad, the surge in the four Dragon economies was driving a correspondingly rapid rise in income per capita, at that time stagnating in China, where two-thirds of the population were still living in extreme poverty. Why shouldn't China be able to do the same as its neighbours, especially as three of them were actually ethnic Chinese? For Deng, the strategy successfully pursued by these small countries (market economies in which priority was given to light industry and a greater openness to the outside world) constituted a radical challenge to the path taken by China since 1949, based on central planning, self-sufficiency and the primacy of heavy industry. He was faced with two ineluctable and inter-linked imperatives that would guide his action from 1978 to 1994: economic efficiency, without any ideological preference as to the means, and uncompromising preservation of political stability through strict Party control of society.[12] Deng employed two strategies to unleash growth in an economy hitherto shackled by centralised control and isolation,[13] namely domestic reform and the expansion of foreign trade. For Deng, however, growth was not an end in itself but a means to achieve a political objective: that of legitimising the domination of the Party-State.

From central planning to market socialism

"I think that there are no fundamental contradictions between a socialist system and a market economy. The question is what method we should use to develop the social forces of production in a more effective way. If we can combine planning and the market economy, I think it will help."

This excerpt from an interview given by Deng Xiaoping to *Time* magazine in 1985[14] sums up the philosophy behind the reforms introduced from 1978 in accordance with the decision taken by the Third Plenary Session of the 11th Central Committee of the CPC, held in December 1978. They were intended to gradually transform a collectivist planned economy into a market economy, leaving plenty of scope for private enterprise. Deng Xiaoping's reforms were both gradual and pragmatic, tested sector by sector, initially on a small scale and then on a larger scale (or not) according to the results, advancing then pausing and sometimes even retreating. During the transition phase, Chinese growth was built on a dual system in which planning instruments coexisted with market mechanisms. It allowed economic operators to adjust gradually until the free-market approach prevailed in almost all sectors. The reforms ushered in three major changes: liberalisation of the production system, industrial diversification and massive urbanisation.

Liberalisation of the production system affected agriculture first, between 1978 and 1984, before reaching the urban industrial sector.[15] The economic revolution began very modestly in 1978 with the trial in certain rural areas of a partial return to family farming. Collectivised in 1955 and organised into people's communes from 1958, the agricultural sector had grown only slowly, at an average annual rate of 2 per cent. In addition to raising farm prices set by the state under the plan, the reform had two other main thrusts: a return to family farming models, which rapidly spread throughout most of rural China, and the possibility for farmers to sell freely any surplus produce in relation to their quotas under the plan. A twin system emerged: whereas at the start of the reform 95 per cent of output was sold at prices set by the state, by 1985 that figure had fallen to 37 per cent, the remainder being sold at market price. Driven by these incentives, agricultural production diversified and grew more than twice as fast as in the previous thirty years (4.5 per cent a year compared with 2 per cent). The success of the agricultural reforms paved the way for a new phase of liberalisation, addressing the means of industrial production, hitherto the preserve of state-owned companies bound by the Plan's restrictive targets.

Being more complex, the process of reform in the industrial and service sectors lasted through the 1980s and 1990s, progressing in the same gradual and parallel way that had proved so successful in the agricultural sector. Step by step, market systems were put into place. Plan norms were relaxed, state companies became financially autonomous, prices and trade were liberalised and public enterprises were restructured or privatised. The reforms also encouraged the creation and development of small businesses in rural areas, their dynamism and rapid productivity gains making a considerable contribution to China's soaring industrial output. More productive farming methods freed up millions of workers for industry, especially as a marked reduction in mortality rates since the start of the Maoist period had resulted in a sharp rise in the labour force. A mass exodus from the countryside brought millions of new workers to the major manufacturing centres. Reforms, together with the influx of additional labour, gave industry a tremendous boost: value-added rose at an annual rate of 12.9 per cent between 1979 and 2008. The heavy industry inherited from the Soviet model still played an important part, but industrial expansion was driven by a wave of renewal and diversification. Traditional industries modernised and new industries emerged, making technologically more sophisticated products such as domestic appliances, cars and electronics. This accelerated industrialisation led to massive urbanisation: the urban population, excluding migrants (*mingong*), tripled in under thirty years, rising from 190 million in 1980 to 607 million in 2009.[16] China now has eighty-nine cities with over a million inhabitants, whereas the United States and India have thirty-seven and thirty-two respectively.

As a result of the reforms and labour force growth, in the space of just thirty years China has become a leading industrial power. Domestic consumption has made a relatively small contribution to growth because of low purchasing power and a high savings ratio. Economic expansion has therefore been driven by exports and, above all, investment, which rose to a record 38 per cent of GDP over the period 1978–2008. The needs were indeed enormous, not only for offices and factories but also for infrastructure and housing needed to cope with the massive urbanisation. Private sector firms, non-existent in 1978, accounted for two-thirds of output in 2008 and were twice as productive as state-owned enterprises.[17] Today, almost the entire economy is regulated by market mechanisms, while price controls have been almost entirely dismantled and now apply to only 5 per cent of goods and services.

This gradual liberalisation of the means of production, accompanied by legal, tax and financial reforms, introduced a new economic system which the 14th Congress defined in 1992 as the "socialist market economy"; the expression was incorporated into the Constitution the following year. A contradiction in terms for free-market economists, this concept linking socialism and the market attempts to provide a theoretical underpinning for an essentially pragmatic approach and expresses China's desire to explore a new way: neither socialist in the Soviet manner nor capitalist along Western lines, it would be the path of Chinese-style socialism.

Globalisation and how to make the most of it

Greater international openness was the keynote of the second round of reforms on which Deng Xiaoping embarked in the late 1970s. Foreign trade was essential to encourage growth, previously stifled by the isolationism of Maoist self-sufficiency. As with domestic reform, the step-by-step approach prevailed, together with a Japanese-style mercantilist policy of protecting the domestic market while promoting exports. China was also anxious to accelerate the process of reducing its technology lag, but it went for a radically different solution from the one chosen in post-war Japan. Whereas Japan preferred to acquire licences, China opted to attract foreign direct investment (FDI), which would play a crucial role in the development of new industries and China's growing integration into regional production systems.

However, gradualism and selectiveness continued to be the key tenets of this new openness, which welcomed foreign firms in a way reminiscent of enclave capitalism. In 1980, low-tax special economic zones (SEZs) for joint ventures with foreign partners[18] were set up in the coastal provinces of Guangdong and Fujian. Authorisations were issued according to the sector concerned, with priority being given to new technologies and export industries. Their success led to the creation of more SEZs in all the coastal regions, followed by the gradual relaxation of the rules covering, for example, the size of foreign shareholdings, factory locations and sectors of activity. The amount of FDI remained relatively small during the 1980s, just a few billion dollars a year, but a turning point came in 1992. The political insecurity that had followed the events of Tiananmen Square had faded and the government opened China's domestic market to foreign investors, who had previously been restricted to export industries. Foreign capital flooded in, at an average of USD 42 billion a year between 1995 and 2000, rising to USD 63 billion a year after China joined the WTO in 2001.[19] Most inward investment came from companies in Hong Kong, Taiwan, Japan and South Korea wanting to relocate some labour-intensive production to China as part of the regional division of labour across Asia.

Openness to foreign investment was accompanied by a liberalisation of foreign trade. These two elements were closely linked, as foreign firms played a key role in China's foreign trade explosion. A two-tier customs system for imports was introduced in the 1980s. Standard tariffs were set very high to protect domestic producers[20] but a preferential regime existed for "processing trade," i.e. imports of intermediate goods to be assembled locally then re-exported. Intended to promote exports, the system allowed China to make the most of its major comparative advantage—cheap labour—and hence to become the workshop of the world, and more specifically of Asian manufacturers. Exports tripled in the 1980s and quadrupled in the following decade. WTO membership gave a further boost to trade, which grew at an annual rate of 25 per cent from 2002, enabling China to overtake Germany as the world's biggest exporter in 2009. In thirty years China's exports rose from USD 18 billion to USD 1.2 trillion. However, this unprecedented success was based not only on China's structural advantages, especially the cost and quality of labour, but also on selective liberalisation of its foreign trade and its successful integration into global production systems. An extremely astute player of the globalisation game, China is undoubtedly the country that has taken best advantage of the phenomenon to move up from the rear of the pack, in economic terms, to the leading group. In thirty years, Beijing's policy of gradual reform enabled China successfully to complete a double transition from a planned economy to a market economy and from self-sufficiency to international integration. However, the fact that reform was gradual does not mean that it proceeded at an even pace over the three decades. The period 1978–1992 saw the first stirrings of liberalisation, but the rate of change accelerated thereafter with the switch to a market economy being seen as the quickest way out of under-development.

Growth as a strategic aim of the Party-State

Rapid liberalisation should not give the illusion that China has converted to free-market capitalism. These developments have nothing in common with the Hegelian vision of historian Francis Fukuyama, for whom the fall of the Berlin wall and the triumph of liberal democracy marked the "end of history." The transition in China has been quite different from the "big bang" in the former Communist countries of Eastern Europe. It is based on the paradoxical concept of the "socialist market economy," coined in order to give credence to the ideological shift begun in 1978 and confirmed in 1992. Marxism-Leninism and Mao's thinking are still honoured, but as relics. For Deng Xiaoping and his successors, China is at the "primary stage of socialism" during which there are two key priorities: prosperity and harmonious development. The purpose of economic growth is to build what Deng termed a "moderately well-off society" (*xia-*

okang shehui), even if some members get rich quicker than others. But the model is also just as much that of a "harmonious society" (*hexie shehui*). Communism is thus pushed aside in favour of the cult of economic performance "in harmony." To promote social harmony, the government would even discreetly reappropriate the heritage of Confucianism,[21] reviled during the Cultural Revolution. A "prosperous and powerful" country (*fuqiang*), a "harmonious society" (*hexie shehui*): these are objectives to inspire national pride, or even nationalist fervour, and the government is skilled in using them to bond society and reinforce its own legitimacy.

Totalitarianism may have ended, but an authoritarian government continues to control civil society, with a more or less heavy hand depending on the period and the issues at stake. The Communist Party of China (CPC) governs on the people's behalf but the Communist ideal has been emptied of all substance. Having lost its ideological legitimacy, the government can hold on to power only by asserting China's might, especially on the economic stage. At the pinnacle of the system, development is a strategic objective of the Party-State. The pursuit of rapid growth, at least equal to that of its neighbours, is essential to bolster the regime's legitimacy, since it underpins the general rise in living standards and the greater influence wielded by the country in the region.

Reforms have been and still are being conducted in a gradual and pragmatic way. However, a thread may be seen running through the two-stage strategy used by the government to first attain and then harness economic power, a priority aim of the Party-State. The first stage, which began in 1978 but really took off after 1992, was to catch up economically and achieve international integration. It has turned China into the world's second-largest economy and biggest exporter. China owes most of its success to the judicious use of the opportunities offered by globalisation. To optimise its integration into the global economy, China has played its trump card: abundant, educated and very cheap labour. The second stage, already under way, is the attainment of scientific and technological excellence. This is where the real contest with Japan will play out over the next twenty years, given that technological superiority is one of Japan's few remaining bastions against China's ambitions.

Japan's resilience

"A rich nation, a strong army" (*fukoku kyōhei*)[22] was the mantra of the reformers who in 1868 transformed Japan from an essentially agricultural country[23] into a great industrial and military power. A new Japan, open to the world and keen to equal the West, was born on 3 January 1868, the day when imperial power was restored in the person of the Meiji emperor. As often in the country's history, it took an external shock to kickstart change and trigger a revolution in all but name. In 1853, an American fleet commanded by Commodore Perry entered Tokyo Bay to demand the opening up to international trade of what had been in effect a closed country for two and a half centuries. In 1858 Japan, like China, had to sign the "unequal treaties" with the Western powers. This humiliation hastened the demise of the Shogunate and the restoration of imperial power.

The Meiji restoration initiated a radical process, motivated by a fierce desire for national independence and economic expansion to Western levels, founded on a strong industrial base, both civilian and military. Manufacturing output increased by a factor of thirty between 1878 and 1939. As the only non-Western industrialised nation, Japan soon joined the great powers in their favourite pursuits, including colonial expansion. That first industrial revolution would sustain Japan's war effort during the conflicts to come and buttress its policy of expansion in Asia.

In 1968, exactly one century after the Meiji restoration, Japan overtook Germany and became the world's third-largest economy after the USA and the Soviet Union. In the meantime, it had won wars resulting in the annexation of Taiwan, Korea and, de facto, Manchuria. This in turn led to the invasion of China but culminated in Japan's first ever defeat, in the Pacific War, and surrender in August 1945. Imperial Japan's ambitions for hegemony in Asia had come to naught, the country lay in ruins and its economy was in tatters, with agricultural and industrial output running at barely a third of their pre-war level. The occupying American administration stepped up the pace of political reform and economic reconstruction, for US strategy was to turn its former enemy into an ally against the Communist threat in the region.[24] Just ten years after its defeat, the newly democratised country embarked on what has been called the Japanese "miracle."[25]

The Japanese "miracle"

High growth and external shocks (1955–1980)

The "miracle" refers to the "High Growth" period (1955–73), when an average annual growth rate of 9.7 per cent was sustained over eighteen years, as compared with the 9.8 per cent achieved by China over the last thirty years. Japanese GDP grew fivefold between 1955 and 1973[26] and doubled between 1974 and 1990. Numerous theories have been put forward to explain this remarkable expansion, some of them questionable on account of their underlying essentialism or culturalism. However, four factors indisputably played a key role: savings, education, the government and private enterprise.[27] Let us look at each one in turn, starting with savings. National savings amounted to 35 per cent of GDP over the period, compared with 23 per cent for OECD countries as a whole. As well as financing the construction of housing and infrastructure, these abundant savings deposits also fuelled massive investment in industry, which subsequently grew at a record annual rate of 15 per cent. Household savings, the biggest share of the total, accounted for 19 per cent of disposable income during the period, compared with 8 per cent in the United States and 12 per cent in France. There are several explanations for such a high savings ratio, among them tax incentives, the cost of housing and education, and scant welfare provision. The second factor, education, played a major role in enabling Japan to adapt to new technologies. In 1960, for example, UNESCO statistics show that the secondary enrolment rate was 74 per cent in Japan compared with 46 per cent in France. The third factor was the government, which acted as a "developer"[28] through two key ministries, the Ministry of Finance (MOF) and the Ministry of International Trade and Industry (MITI). MOF administered and oversaw a financial system programmed for industrial expansion; MITI regulated competition, supported exports and steered industrial production towards the most promising sectors in terms of technological progress and global demand. The fourth factor was private enterprise, whether in the shape of giant conglomerates (*keiretsu*) or countless small businesses. This dual structure kept the industrial fabric flexible, while a high-quality labour force enabled firms to move rapidly up the technological ladder and constantly evolve organisational methods to ensure high productivity. Abundant savings deposits, high-quality education, state support and competitive, export-oriented industry all played key roles in Japan's accelerating industrialisation. Two other factors also came into play: the country's determination to catch up with the United States and the exceptional political stability that came with the unbroken rule of the conservative Liberal Democratic Party.

In 1974, a double whammy sent the economy into a savage recessionary spiral. The 1973 oil shock quadrupled oil prices and hit Japan at its most vulnerable point, energy dependence, while exports were undermined by the appreciation of the yen, which rose by over 30 per cent in two years. Annual inflation rose to 25 per cent in 1974 and a period of adjustment became necessary. Household savings financed budget stimulus packages, while the quest for energy efficiency brought about profound changes in production methods. Growth resumed at an annual rate of 4 per cent until the end of the 1970s, by which time Japan was the world's third-largest economy and third-largest exporter with 6.4 per cent of the global market in 1980, compared with 2.1 per cent in 1955. Japan was ready for the next phase of its expansion.

Rivalling the United States (1980–1989)

The Japanese giant still lacked two essential elements in its quest to become a global economic superpower: technological supremacy and financial dominance. Government policies during the 1980s were determined by this twin goal. At the start of the decade, even though Japan devoted the same proportion of its resources to research and development (R&D) as the United States, priority was given to applied research and product development. Japan's deficiency in fundamental research was evidenced by the small number of Japanese articles published and cited in academic literature worldwide. For the government, technological innovation was the key to international competitiveness and the 1980s were declared the "decade of technology," the embodiment being Expo '85, the International Exposition held at Tsukuba in 1985. MITI launched two long-term fundamental research programmes in 1981, though without abandoning what had been so beneficial to the country until then, namely the optimisation of industrial processes and the development of new products. In semi-conductors, for example, Toshiba developed the first 256K memory chip in 1983, followed by a 1024K chip in 1985. Major Japanese manufacturers like Toshiba, NEC and Hitachi would dominate the global market for many years. The same applied to liquid-crystal displays (LCDs). Although Japanese researchers had gained little international recognition and the number of Japanese Nobel Prize winners remained small, by the end of the decade Japan had made up most of its deficit in relation to the United States: it generated more patents in relation to the size of its economy than any other country in the world.

Its second goal was financial dominance and here again the savings ratio played a key role. Savings deposits had successively financed the enormous investments required for industrial expansion and the budget deficits of the 1970s. During the 1980s, the excess of savings over domestic investment sustained a rising balance of payments surplus that would further fuel international financial expansion. Having gained a technological and commercial lead in many fields, Japan was now threatening America's financial supremacy. Japan's rise as a financial power during the decade was almost perfectly symmetrical with America's decline. Japan, the world's largest creditor nation, was accumulating substantial foreign assets and running both a balance of payments and a budget surplus, while its financial institutions were expanding internationally. The United States, now the world's biggest debtor nation, was seeing its foreign debt rise sharply and running both a balance of payments and a budget deficit, while its financial institutions were retrenching. Two figures sum up the scale of this shift in the balance of financial power towards Japan: an American balance of payments deficit of USD 880 billion between 1981 and 1990 and a Japanese surplus of USD 441 billion over the same period. The growing surplus drove the financial expansion of all the different players in the Japanese economy. Tokyo overtook New York as the world's biggest stock market in 1987, the world's ten biggest banks in 1989 were all Japanese and were responsible for 30 per cent of all international lending, while the government had doubled the amount of its overseas development assistance in four years and through its financial contributions was wielding growing influence in international organisations.

Japanese companies in the non-financial sector were not left behind. The massive financial firepower at their disposal enabled them to internationalise at the double, investing in productivity at home while expanding abroad. By 1989, Japan had become the world's biggest investor, even buying up American icons such as the Rockefeller Center, CBS Records and MCA Universal. The 1980s were golden years, and by 1989 it looked as though nothing could halt Japan's stellar ascension as an industrial, technological and financial power, increasingly threatening American supremacy in a global game of catch-as-catch-can. On the financial front, however, America still had the ultimate weapon of the dollar and was able to impose a substantial revaluation of the yen in the September 1985 Plaza Accord. Washington may have counted the near doubling in value of the yen against the dollar between 1985 and 1987 a victory but it was to prove a pyrrhic one: the delayed effect of such a brutal adjustment was to plunge Japan into a crisis that would have fateful consequences not only for that country but for the global economy as a whole.

Crisis and renewal

The 1990s: a lost decade?

Pride comes before a fall: after the glorious decade of the 1980s, Japan was to endure ten years of financial, economic and systemic crisis. What caused this sudden plunge into what is generally known as the "lost decade"? There were two drivers of financial expansion in the 1980s. The first was the accumulation of a massive foreign trade surplus due to the competitiveness of Japanese products; the second was a speculative bubble caused by the near doubling in value of the yen and the lax monetary policy subsequently introduced to counter its effects. The bubble burst in 1990 and the ensuing collapse of stock market and real estate prices, which had tripled since 1985, triggered a financial meltdown. Poor crisis management by the government led to bank insolvencies that threatened the entire Japanese financial system. The crisis spread into the real economy: growth rates ran at barely 1 per cent a year on average during the decade and unemployment doubled.

The government used the twin levers of budget and monetary policy to deal with the problem. Ten stimulus plans followed in rapid succession over the ten-year period, at a total cost of USD 1 trillion, but they had such little effect that interest rates were cut to almost zero. Despite this shock treatment the recovery failed to materialise. In fact, the financial crisis and subsequent recession revealed a deeper, systemic crisis linked to the unsuitability of a socio-economic model which, having been the source of Japan's success, was now hampering its resurgence. Unlike competitive Anglo-Saxon capitalism, Japanese capitalism had a Germanic "corporatist" cast, insofar as it was based on community of interests. At company level, solidarity existed between individual members of conglomerates, between banks and businesses, between employees and employers. At economic policy level, in a model where the state played a leading role in development, converging interests meant that the "iron triangle" of government, civil service and business was closely involved in setting policy objectives and determining how to achieve them. During the 1990s, recession and the effects of globalisation shook this structure to its foundations and the inter-relationships of the "iron triangle" fell apart. The political class and the civil service lost credibility, partly as a result of a series of scandals but mostly because of their inability to forestall the crisis. Social cohesion and egalitarianism, a source of pride in Japan, crumbled. The previous advantages of the system were now bringing the country to its knees.

And yet the 1990s were not a lost decade. In the financial sector, where the crisis had begun, far-reaching reforms were introduced, independent supervisory bodies were set up and there was a shakeout in the banking system. Big firms restructured in order to make better use of their financial and human capital and a new generation of entrepreneurs emerged, imbued with the innovating drive of the post-war years. More generally, Japanese society as a whole may well have changed more in the 1990s than in the forty-five years since the end of the war, becoming less monolithic. Its traditional characteristics of respect for authority and devotion to the group gradually gave way to new values centred more on the individual, such as self-fulfilment and the creative urge. Far from being a decade of sterility, the 1990s paved the way for the future.

A third round of modernisation?

After a succession of ten prime ministers during the crisis years, Junichiro Koizumi took power in April 2001. The Japanese were looking for a strong leader and he certainly represented a break with the past, with his non-conformist style, his campaign[29] and the composition of his government, more open to women and to civil society. He set out his stall as soon as he was appointed: Japan had to change because there would be no economic growth or renewal without drastic structural measures. The goal was now to turn Japan into the world's leading knowledge economy. During his five years in office he embarked with stubborn determination on a series of reforms that seemed to set Japan on the road to another round of modernisation, the third after the Meiji and post-war reforms. A thorough shakeout in the banking sector, budgetary rigour, the redirection of resources towards social protection and promising sectors for the future, privatisation of public enterprises and the Post Office, support for innovation: painful and often ill-received, the measures were nevertheless necessary for Japan's productive system to adapt to the new challenges posed by international competition.[30] At the same time, China's accession to the WTO set off a surge in trade, especially with Japan. The Japanese economy recovered at last and entered a new cycle, growing at an average annual rate of 2 per cent from 2003 to 2007. Koizumi's record was mixed when his term came to an end in 2006: budgetary rigour and renewed growth through structural reforms on the upside, but greater social inequality at home and a sharp deterioration in diplomatic relations with Japan's Asian neighbours, especially China, on the downside. His departure also marked the end of a period of stability for the government: the third round of modernisation that had been taking shape stalled as three prime ministers came and went before the elections in August 2009. A political earthquake, the Democratic Party's assumption of power in September 2009, held out the hope of a genuine modernisation of Japan's economy, social structures and institutions. However, it is to be feared that the change of prime minister in June 2010 and the DPJ's defeat in the Upper House elections on 11 July will further delay the necessary reforms.

Interlinked fates

China's awakening, Japan's resilience: the paths taken by the two countries over the last thirty years may seem unconnected or even divergent. Yet they are linked by certain similarities in their economic models and by a sediment of memories laid down during a long and troubled relationship.

Economic convergence

Whatever the differences in their political systems, a high degree of convergence is apparent in their growth models. Of course, China can point to the unique nature of its development experience, but the way the economy has caught up since 1978 has much in common with Japan's initial stirrings during the Meiji period and industrial expansion in the period 1955–73. Whether in China's thirty golden years or Japan's high-growth era, the

27

same four elements (savings, education, government, private enterprise) played the same key roles. There are some differences, however. The first is to be found in the classic growth factors of labour, capital and technological innovation. The twin drivers of Japan's high-growth period were capital investment and technological progress; labour made a negligible contribution since there was virtually no increase in the labour force or the number of hours worked. Investment was also the main driver of growth during China's thirty golden years but labour made a greater contribution than technological progress, for employment grew by 2 per cent a year whereas technological progress advanced more slowly. Another difference with Japan was the role of the state: as well as acting as a "developer" through government policy, the Chinese state played an entrepreneurial role through its direct involvement in the productive system, since the state sector still accounts for a third of domestic output.[31] The two models show similarities in foreign relations and in their approach to globalisation, since both are determined by a neo-mercantilist approach, which protects the domestic market and promotes exports, leveraged at certain times by an undervalued currency. Yet striking differences exist in two specific areas. First, China considers openness to foreign investment as the quickest way to make up its technology lag. Conversely, Japan has always preferred to acquire foreign technologies in order to protect its own market and safeguard its socio-economic system. The door has opened just a crack since the mid-1990s but the stock of foreign investment still represents only 3.6 per cent of GDP compared with 9 per cent in China, 15 per cent in the United States and 35 per cent in France. Second, China, which does not yet have a large domestic market, is also much more open to international trade. Exports rose from 20 per cent of GDP in the 1990s to an average of 32 per cent since China joined the WTO, compared with less than 10 per cent for Japan in the 1960s and 1970s.

But whatever the differences, the models that underpin the economic "miracles" in Japan from 1955 to 1973 and in China from 1978 to 2008 have many common features: still largely administered economies, educated labour forces, low wages, abundant personal savings fuelling industrial investment, selective openness to international trade and, above all, a common national resolve to gain economic supremacy and thereby erase past humiliations.

Five key steps in a troubled history

The paths taken by the two empires have intersected on many occasions. Here, we will look briefly at five key steps that have had a structural influence on Japan's relations with China and, consciously or not, have deeply marked the national psyche. Kinship, emancipation, "betrayal," aggression, recognition: making allowance for a rather broad-brush approach, the troubled history of Sino-Japanese relations may be summed up in these five key steps.

Kinship

The first key step is Japan's religious and cultural kinship with China. Mahâyâna ("great vehicle") Buddhism and Confucianism spread to Japan from China via Korea in the sixth century. Through these movements Japan came under the cultural sway of the Middle Empire, from which it borrowed ideograms, institutions and social etiquette. In 645, the Taika Reform Edicts introduced the Chinese administrative model into Japan in order to organise the political system (*ritsuryō*). The matrix of this mother culture would shape the Japanese people's linguistic, artistic and spiritual universe, though they adapted the heritage to their existing cultural environment and enhanced it over the centuries with many original contributions of their own.

Emancipation

A second turning point came in the sixteenth century and concerned the Hua-Yi tribute-based system which regulated China's relations with its neighbours.[32] In the imperial cosmogony, China was placed under heaven; it stood at the centre of the world and therefore represented the only civilised place. The emperor was the Son of Heaven and it was in Heaven's name that he ruled as monarch over his subjects. Neighbouring countries, being barbarian, could only be his vassals and he their natural sovereign, always in Heaven's name. Hegel perceived this order as set and immobile, concluding that China had, as it were, removed itself from the course of history since only the sovereign was free.[33] Peace and the development of trade depended on the tributary system imposed on neighbouring countries, especially Korea, Vietnam, Burma and the *Ryūkyū* archipelago. Regulating international relations between the centre and the periphery hierarchically, it represented China's assertion of an ontological superiority that was both cultural and moral. Japan clearly rejected Chinese suzerainty, paying tribute only for a short period in the fifteenth century and refusing any form of allegiance or subservience to China in the following century.[34] Japan's non-participation in the Asian tributary system and constant rejection of Chinese hegemony was to be of crucial importance for the future development of Sino-Japanese relations.

Betrayal?

A third key step in Sino-Japanese relations was the Meiji restoration of 1868. Critical for modernisation, it also signified Japan's choice of Western modernity over Chinese tradition, interpreted by some in China as a kind of betrayal. The phrase coined by Yukichi Fukuzawa, the most influential Japanese intellectual of the time and founder of Keio University, did not beat about the bush: *Datsu-A, Nyu-O* ("Leave Asia, Join Europe").

In an unsigned article[35] he denounced the inertia of a China that clung to an age-old conservatism sustained by a superficial reading of Confucius and refused to embrace progress. Meiji Japan's choice of the West was not limited to technical and economic progress, since it also included the colonial strategy that the great powers were implementing in the region. Fukuzawa even saw Japan's victory over China in 1895 as a "victory for civilisation over barbarism," a somewhat surprising reversal of roles in view of the tributary system mentioned earlier.

In fact, far from being a "betrayal" of China, the Meiji restoration would inspire the nationalist revolution that led to the overthrow of the Qing dynasty in 1911. At the turn of the century, nationalist students and intellectuals who had fled to Japan found political, media and financial support there. Sun Yat-sen founded a nationalist republican party, the forerunner of the Kuomintang, in Tokyo in 1905. For the Chinese revolutionaries seeking to end China's political deliquescence and make up its economic deficit, Japan was if not a model at least a source of inspiration.

Aggression

The fourth and most dramatic episode in this troubled relationship was the second Sino-Japanese war (1937–45). Japan's aggression and the crimes it committed continue to weigh heavily on relations between the two countries to this day. The first war between them in 1894–95 had ended with Japanese victory and the Treaty of Shimonoseki, under which China ceded Taiwan to Japan and recognised the independence of Korea, which Japan annexed in 1910. Japanese expansionism in Asia continued during the 1930s, motivated in particular by the Empire's need for raw materials. In 1931, the Imperial Army invaded Manchuria and established a puppet state, Manchukuo. In July 1937, seizing the opportunity presented by a minor incident it may have intentionally provoked, Japan invaded northern China, took Beijing and fought bloody battles at Shanghai and Nanking. The massacre that followed the fall of Nanking in December 1937 was the worst atrocity of the invasion. By 1939, Japanese forces occupied the whole of north-eastern China and a large portion of its coastal areas.[36]

Recognition

The fifth key step was recognition. This was evidenced in Japan's diplomatic recognition of the People's Republic of China (PRC) in 1972 and, at a more general level, in the mutual recognition of two near neighbours with no hegemonic ambitions enshrined in the 1978 Peace and Friendship Treaty, still in force.

Tokyo's recognition of the PRC was by no means a foregone conclusion. Earlier, on 8 September 1951, a defeated Japan signed the San Francisco Treaty with the Allies, followed by another treaty under which the United States undertook to guarantee Japanese security. Sovereignty was restored the following year and Japan concluded a peace treaty with nationalist China which, in accordance with the American position, was the only part of China it recognised. Trade relations developed with both Chinas but the Japanese political class was split between pro-Peking and pro-Taipei factions. In 1971, Henry Kissinger secretly met China's leaders in Peking and announced that President Nixon would visit the People's Republic the following year. Japan, which had not been informed of the contacts, was wrongfooted by Washington's U-turn; it was the first "Nixon shock," as the Japanese press called it. A second was shortly to follow, falling, as chance would have it, on the anniversary of Japan's surrender in 1945. On 15 August 1971, Nixon unexpectedly took the dollar off the gold standard, ushering in the start of a new monetary system, full of menace for the Japanese economy. Japan's trust in its American protector was badly shaken; Tokyo decided to take up its own position on the Chinese question and made overtures to Beijing. Negotiations made rapid progress and Japan recognised the People's Republic of China in 1972, six years before the United States. The two countries issued a joint communiqué, paragraph 7 of which is worth quoting: "The normalisation of relations between Japan and China is not directed against any third country. Neither of the two countries should seek hegemony in the Asia-Pacific region and each is opposed to efforts by any other country or group of countries to establish such hegemony." The communiqué called for the signing of a Peace and Friendship Treaty, which would take six more years to draft because of China's insistence on the inclusion of the non-hegemony clause. Tokyo finally acquiesced and the treaty was signed in 1978. Opinion polls in Japan in the 1980s endorsed the rapprochement, with 70 per cent of the population expressing a favourable opinion of China. Twenty years later the situation had been turned on its head: since the turn of the century, the prevailing mood in both Japan and China has been one of mistrust, antipathy and hostility. Have old grievances resurfaced? The recognition process had doubtless not been fully worked through. Formal recognition treaties had been concluded in the interests of diplomatic pragmatism, but the darker moments of the two countries' shared history had been swept under the carpet.

These five key steps in a troubled history illustrate the two countries' linked destinies in a dialectical movement of fascination and resentment that continues to influence their relations. Though its cultural and moral universe still bears the imprint of imperial China, from the outset Japan rejected any dependence on its larger neighbour with its universalist pretensions. On the contrary, it took advantage of China's momentary weakness to invade the country, asserting its own hegemonic ambitions. That invasion and the atrocities committed in its wake remain deeply ingrained in the Chinese psyche to this day.

2

MIGHTY BUT VULNERABLE

Between them, the two Asian giants represent 77 per cent of output in East Asia and 15 per cent of global GDP. With a staggered start of twenty years, their economic expansion has followed a similar track, based on massive industrialisation financed by abundant domestic savings deposits. But for all their industrial might, they are also vulnerable. As it happened in Japan in the 1990s, the global crisis in 2008–09 revealed weaknesses that could constrain their potential for growth.

The levers of economic power

Although it has a different political system, China is pursuing the same three-phase strategy employed by the Japanese to get their hands on the levers of economic power. The first phase involves developing a competitive industrial base. This paves the way for the second phase, the rapid expansion of foreign trade, which in turn generates a substantial foreign trade surplus. In the third phase, the accumulated surpluses unlock the door to financial power. The difference between the paths taken by the two protagonists lies in the driving force behind their industrial competitiveness: in Japan the superiority of its product technology, in China the abundance of cheap labour.

China's immense potential

The world's second-largest industrial power, China became the largest trading nation in 2009. The rapidity of China's ascension to financial heights is due to the accumulation of a massive trade surplus, even though Japan remains by far the world's largest creditor nation. If the spectacular industrial, commercial and financial achievements of the first decade of the twenty-first century are anything to go by, China's economic expansion is likely to continue for the next twenty years because it has vast potential for further growth.

The world's second-largest industrial power

The importance of the secondary sector, especially manufacturing industry, which accounts for 35 per cent of GDP, reflects China's position as the "workshop" of Asia and the world. It has overtaken Japan to become the world's second-largest industrial power, accounting for 12 per cent of global value-added; yet as recently as 2000, China's industrial sector was only a third the size of Japan's.

Just as there was no Japanese "miracle" there is no Chinese "miracle." In both cases the strategy was the same: government policies that enabled human and financial resources to be channelled into industrial expansion, the necessary huge investments being funded by abundant domestic savings deposits. For a low-income country, China has a quite remarkable level of gross savings: they have risen steadily since 2005 and now exceed 50 per cent of GDP. Supplemented by foreign investment, savings deposits are financing a monumental investment effort that gathered pace through the 1990s and 2000s to reach 48 per cent of GDP in 2009. Even Japan and the other Dragons were not able to match this achievement in a comparable timeframe.

Why is China growing so fast? Principally, because the Chinese are investing vast amounts. The contribution of foreign capital,[1] though substantial in absolute terms,[2] is still small in relation to the torrent of industrial investment by Chinese firms. However, that investment is crucial if China is to bridge the technology gap and is essential for exports, as foreign firms are the source of more than half of China's exports, especially in cutting-edge sectors.[3]

As well as being the world's biggest producer of coal, steel, aluminium, cement and fertiliser, China is a leader in several traditional light industries such as textiles, toys and footwear. It is also looming increasingly large in more sophisticated segments such as domestic appliances, televisions, computers and cars. The types of product that companies manufacture are largely determined by their location and by whether they are state- or privately-owned. State companies, mostly located in the northern provinces and primarily engaged in heavy industry, account for 35 per cent of output against over 80 per cent in 1978. The coastal provinces attract foreign firms and private or "collective" Chinese companies specialising in traditional light industries or new industries such as electronics and cars.

China has become a leading maker and exporter of information and communication technology (ICT) products. At least 50 per cent of the world's computers and DVD and MP3 players are made in China. It is here, in consumer and business electronics, that the term "workshop of the world" is most apposite. Asian multinationals, followed by their Western counterparts, have segmented their production processes and relocated them to specific Asian countries according to their individual comparative advantages. China is the obvious choice for labour-intensive final assembly because it has abundant, skilled and cheap labour. As the linchpin of the regional division of labour in Asia, China has become the leading exporter of electronic goods. However, this achievement comes with two caveats: first, there is relatively little value-added in the assembly processes carried out in China; second, foreign firms account for 70 per cent of output and 85 per cent of exports although they represent less than 30 per cent of Chinese industry as a whole.

As in electronics, foreign investors have played a crucial role in developing China's automobile industry, though the government has obliged them to partner local firms in order to lay the foundations of a national industry. Despite the inherent difficulties of such partnerships, all the big-name carmakers are present on a market with vast potential: from an estimated 50 million at the end of 2008, the number of cars in China could triple by 2020. The achievements are remarkable: car making has increased tenfold since 2000 and China has risen from 14th place to become the world's largest producer in 2009.[4] Automobile production in 2009 rose by 48 per cent in comparison with 2008 despite the global crisis and increased by a further 32 per cent in 2010: total output, including commercial vehicles, amounted to 18.2 million units in 2010, compared with 9.3 million in 2008. There was a spectacular jump in passenger car production in particular, from 6.7 million in 2008 to 10.4 million in 2009 and 13.9 million in 2010. Substantial tax incentives have made the Chinese car market the world's largest, ahead of the United States, though the twenty-five or so co-enterprises created by foreign carmakers, Volkswagen and General Motors foremost among them, still account for over 60 per cent of output.

However, domestic brands like Chery and Geely are making headway and starting to export. China has a dual aim in the automobile sector: to supply the domestic market without recourse to imports and to use a solid domestic base as a platform for exports. The current position is somewhere between the two: local production has been sufficient to meet domestic demand since 2006 and China has become a net exporter of cars, albeit in small volumes. Output of passenger cars is likely to soar over the next few years, rising from 13.9 million in 2010 to over 20 million in 2014, substantially exceeding domestic demand. So there is likely to be a formidable international offensive in the next ten years, as was the case with Japan in the mid-1970s. It will be supported by greater technological sophistication, partly achieved through foreign acquisitions. Jockeying for position has already begun, as can be seen from the acquisition of marques like Rover, some of Saab's assets and, above all, the flagship purchase of Volvo in 2009.[5] On the domestic market, the emergence of entirely homegrown carmakers like Chery, Geely and Brilliance is the biggest threat to foreign producers in the medium-term. When foreign technology is reckoned to have penetrated deeply enough into China's industrial fabric, it will be tempting indeed for the government to transform these firms into the champions of a purely national automobile industry. The 2009 revitalisation plan already contained measures to promote concentration in this strategic sector with the aim of rapidly producing two or three leaders capable of making several million cars a year.

The policy of favouring national champions has been at work in other sectors since the 1990s, following a similar strategy to that of Japan's MITI twenty years earlier. That is the case not only in sectors vital to the country's economic security, such as energy, but also in competitive industries. Baosteel (steel), Haier (domestic appliances), TCL (televisions) and Lenovo (computers) are to be found alongside the oil giants Sinopec, CNPC and CNOOC. Their international growth strategy is primarily driven by the massive expansion of exports, but it does not rule out acquiring foreign competitors (Thomson's television division for TCL, IBM's PC division for Lenovo, etc.) or even building factories in other countries (Baosteel in Brazil, Haier in the United States).

Irresistible commercial expansion

China overtook Germany as the world's leading exporter in 2009, with a market share of nearly 9 per cent as against just 2.6 per cent in 1993.[6] Exports, 95 per cent of which are manufactured goods, increased more than sixfold between 2000 and

2010. This phenomenal growth in trade is due to China's successful integration into the globalisation process, crowned by accession to the WTO in 2001. It is based on three closely linked factors: China's key role as an assembly platform, the major contribution of foreign firms to exports and, above all, cheap labour. Wages in China are more than fifteen times lower than in developed countries;[7] unsurprisingly, Chinese industry is exceptionally competitive on the global market for labour-intensive goods.

The contribution of foreign companies has greatly changed the structure of exports, 45 per cent of which are now in the plant and equipment sector. High-tech products account for 30 per cent of exports, compared with 7 per cent in 1995.[8] But although exports of electronic goods have soared, there has not been an equivalent rise up the technology ladder, since sophisticated components are still largely imported. Products exported under the "Made in China" label, like Toshiba or Dell computers, are not strictly speaking "made" there, but merely assembled from imported components. Exempt from duty under processing trade rules, these components account for about 40 per cent of total imports. Raw materials are the other major import item, and the fastest growing. China was self-sufficient in oil until 1993 but now depends on the international market for 50 per cent of its consumption; oil imports have risen sixfold in ten years.

In geographical terms more than half of China's foreign trade is with Asia, but the United States, Japan and Europe are its key export markets. The importance of trade with Asia—47 per cent of exports, 66 per cent of imports[9]—confirms China's pivotal role in the zone's commercial integration. Europe accounts for 22 per cent of Chinese exports and only 14 per cent of imports but the trade imbalance with the United States is even more marked: 21 and 8 per cent respectively. The balance swings the other way with Japan, which accounts for 19 per cent of Chinese exports but 21 per cent of imports (including Hong Kong). Japan may be running a surplus, but the deficits of Europe and the United States have more than tripled since 2000, reaching EUR 169 billion and USD 273 billion respectively in 2010. This deterioration in the balance of trade which, seen from Brussels and above all Washington, calls for a revaluation of the yuan, weighs heavily on relations with Beijing. It also illustrates broader global financial imbalances, with insufficient savings deposits in the United States far outweighed by excess deposits in Asia.

An emerging financial power

As with Japan in the 1980s, China has quickly emerged as a player to be reckoned with on the financial stage because surplus domestic savings deposits are recycled to other countries: China exports capital as well as manufactured goods. Springing from accumulated current account surpluses, China's financial might demonstrates the firepower of the State, financial institutions and businesses, but does not in any way reflect the situation of its households, whose income lies between that of El Salvador and Egypt. The current account surplus peaked at USD 436 billion in 2008, or 9.5 per cent of GDP. That is an extraordinary figure for a large emerging country:[10] in Japan, a developed country, the surplus never exceeded 3.3 per cent of GDP, even at the height of its financial expansion.

China had net foreign assets (minus debt) of a little over USD 1.8 trillion in 2009, or 37 per cent of GDP. Official foreign currency reserves have increased by a factor of fifteen since 2000 due to mounting current account surpluses and inflows of foreign investment. Those reserves, the world's biggest, amounted to USD 2.85 trillion in December 2010, almost triple the size of Japan's, at just over USD 1 trillion.[11] It is estimated that over two-thirds are invested in dollar-denominated securities, includ-

41

ing USD 1,160 billion in US Treasuries at end-2010. China is thus America's leading foreign creditor, holding about 25 per cent of its external government debt, followed by Japan with 20 per cent (USD 886 billion).

There is a downside to investing these surpluses in sovereign assets: the low yields on these bonds will not offset the foreign exchange losses that will eventually flow from the yuan's inevitable appreciation against the dollar. That is what lay behind the creation in September 2007 of a sovereign-wealth fund, China Investment Corporation (CIC). Initially endowed with USD 200 billion, its task is to invest some of China's foreign currency reserves in higher-yielding assets. Some fear that this official role may conceal another objective and that the CIC will become a Trojan horse for takeovers in strategic sectors abroad, such as energy and high technology.[12] China's newly gained financial clout is also reflected in a jump in Chinese foreign direct investment, which rose from USD 3 billion in 2003 to USD 44 billion in 2009. For the time being most investment is concentrated in the raw material and energy sectors, especially in Africa, Latin America and Central Asia. However, a more proactive industrial policy is gradually taking shape, as in Japan during the 1980s. Although considerable resources are directed towards industrial champions looking to expand abroad, they are not the only beneficiaries: Chinese banks have been actively—though not always judiciously—acquiring stakes in their foreign rivals.[13] But there is still a long way to go before China becomes a fully-fledged financial power. It does not yet have a competitive banking system, efficient capital markets or, above all, a currency that can play an international role comparable to that of the yen. The yuan, now convertible for commercial transactions, is not convertible for capital transactions, a factor that hampers its use in international business and limits China's influence in the financial sphere.

Considerable potential for growth

China's economic performance over the last ten years has been remarkable, but what potential for growth does it have over the next two decades? Its own natural resources are already insufficient to satisfy its industry's voracious appetite for energy and raw materials. Imports are soaring and China is becoming more dependent on other countries, since security of supply is closely linked to geopolitical stability. But despite these constraints, two key factors ensure that the country has considerable growth potential: abundant savings deposits and vast resources of labour.

The high savings ratio has financed industrial investment, the locomotive of growth, and since the early 2000s has even exceeded investment needs. It is paradoxical that these excess funds should have been exported in the form of direct or financial investment, since the country still has colossal domestic needs, especially in infrastructure and welfare provision. The growth model will inevitably have to be adapted to strike a better balance between investment and consumption, between commercial expansion abroad and development of the domestic market.[14] Will latent savings be sufficient to continue driving high levels of growth? Gross corporate and household deposits now exceed 50 per cent of GDP: the high profits of Chinese companies (about 20 per cent of GDP) are largely reinvested because dividend payouts are low, while households save nearly 25 per cent of their disposable income. Demographics may partly explain why the ratio is so high, bearing in mind China's one-child policy, but several more specific factors encourage precautionary or accumulation savings, such as tax incentives, the very low level of welfare provision, the cost of education and aspirations to home ownership.

How would things look in 2025 if universal welfare provision was introduced and the growth model was redirected towards domestic consumption? According to available estimates,[15] growth would remain vigorous (8 per cent a year to 2015, then

6.5 per cent), investment would fall back to 30 per cent of GDP from its current level of 48 per cent and private consumption, sustained by the tens of millions of people entering the middle class each year, would surge to 60 per cent of GDP.[16] The foreign trade surplus would be reduced, though it would still amount to 5 per cent of GDP. So even after introducing a less export-oriented economic model, the savings ratio would still be high enough to ensure robust growth.

Turning to the second factor, under-employed rural inhabitants and young graduates also represent sources of labour for what could be termed a dual "reserve army," extending Marx's concept to embrace the net surplus of workers, unemployed or not, at either end of the skill spectrum. According to UN forecasts, the working-age population, which had risen from 600 million in 1980 to 900 million in 2000, will peak at 980 million in 2015 before falling sharply on account of the one-child policy. The largest reserves of labour are currently to be found among the urban unemployed and, even more, the rural under-employed. The official urban unemployment rate is around 4–5 per cent, but the Chinese Academy of Social Sciences (CASS) puts the figure at over 10 per cent.[17] Under-employment is endemic in the countryside due to the seasonal nature of work and the small amount of land allocated to each family, about 0.4 hectare (1 acre) per farmer compared with 30 hectares (75 acres) in France. The redeployment of some 150 million virtually unemployed rural inhabitants into more productive sectors will result in substantial migration and sweeping urbanisation.[18] Higher skill levels will generate productivity gains throughout the economy, as most of the new labour market entrants will have had ten years of schooling compared with four or five for those leaving the labour force. Over 100 million young people are currently in secondary education[19] and 25 million in higher education, 600,000 of them outside China.[20] The number of university graduates each year has increased fivefold since 2000 to 5.6 million, more than half of them engineers and scientists. China produces more engineers than the United States—350,000 a year compared with 137,000, according to a study by Duke University[21]—and almost as many researchers (1 million compared with 1.4 million).

So this dual "reserve army" of under-employed rural inhabitants and young graduates gives China vast reserves of both labour and skill. Not only should its economy benefit from a labour surplus over the next fifteen years or so,[22] but the working population will be increasingly highly skilled. Savings and labour will continue to be important resources but ongoing structural reforms will be necessary in order to optimise their contribution to growth. This involves adjusting the growth model to boost consumption, allocating investment more efficiently to productive sectors and, as a corollary, reorganising a State-run industrial sector that still keeps too many unprofitable firms on life-support.

Japan's strength and agility

Despite having virtually no raw materials and only 2.2 per cent of the world's labour force as against China's 27 per cent, Japan produces as much as its giant neighbour: about 8 per cent of world GDP. This simple fact says much about an economic colossus that combines industrial competitiveness with commercial vigour and financial power.

An industrial and technological heavyweight

Japan's industrial and technological prowess remains its trump card. Unlike China, Japan has already entered the post-industrial era, becoming a knowledge economy: industry accounts for only 26.5 per cent of GDP, services for 72 per cent. Yet Japan is still a top-tier industrial power, in third place behind the United States and China with a 10 per cent share of the global value-added manufacturing sector. Twenty-seven per cent of the labour force is employed in industry and to the 17 million workers in manufacturing and construction can be added 350,000 industrial robots, 45 per cent of the world total. Highly automated production processes use 350 robots for 10,000 employees, compared with 160 in Germany and barely 70 in the United States. Post-war industry was rebuilt and expanded in successive waves—light industry, heavy industry and cutting-edge industries—according to the "flying geese paradigm" developed by the economist Kaname Akamatsu in the mid-1930s. This theory describes the three stages in the development of a product or sector: the product is imported in return for exports of raw materials, then local production replaces imports, and finally the product is exported on a large scale when the domestic market is saturated. The cycle is renewed as the country climbs the technology ladder.[23] One of the many factors underlying the success of Japanese industry was the strategy implemented under the aegis of MITI, based on the selective targeting of products with substantial technological value-added and strong global demand. That is why Japan is at the forefront of the automobile industry, on a par with the United States, accounting for 16 per cent of global output and almost double that figure if the output of Japanese carmakers in other countries is included. Japan is the world leader in machine tools and industrial robots, ahead of Germany and second in steelmaking (though a long way behind China) and shipbuilding (behind South Korea). It leads the field in some of the most advanced segments of electronics and biotechnologies and is preparing the technologies of the future in optronics, home automation, nanotechnologies,[24] neurosciences, new materials, etc. However, highly selective targeting is not without its downside: Japan is weak in pharmaceuticals, aerospace and agri-food, for example.

Two pillars support this offensive strategy: the abandonment or relocation of unprofitable activities and permanent innovation in buoyant industries. Japan has always taken a very cautious approach to relocation, fearing the hollowing-out of its industry.[25] However, it has not hesitated to abandon certain segments and relocate others as soon as raw materials prices, wage costs or exchange rates made production costs prohibitive in Japan. Relocating unprofitable industries does not generally mean entirely withdrawing from the sector concerned, since production in Japan tends to move higher up the value chain (professional textiles, carbon fibre, special steels, drilling platforms, floating factories, etc.). It is still in automotive production and cutting-edge technologies that Japan's cost-efficient, innovative and agile industrial base comes into its own. With no natural resources to speak of and subject to fierce competition from its Asian neighbours, Japan has no alternative but to innovate in response to the challenge from China.[26]

Commercial vigour and internationalisation

Japan's share of world exports has shrunk considerably over the last ten years, falling from 8 to 5 per cent. At the same time, China's share has almost doubled, from 5 to 9 per cent. But although slowing, Japan is still the world's fourth-largest exporter, drawing its commercial strength first and foremost from the composition of its trade, which gives it a structural surplus. Running a deficit in raw materials, energy and agri-food, it has a substantial surplus in high value-added manufactured goods, which make up 98 per cent of its exports. Its comparative advantages are concentrated in capital-intensive goods with a high research input. Three sectors alone account for 65 per cent of Japan's exports: automobiles (25 per cent), electrical machinery (20 per cent) and other capital goods such as machine tools (20 per cent).

The structure of Japan's export trade varies from one region to another. The United States, for example, takes 17 per cent of

Japanese exports overall but 33 per cent of its automobile exports, which explains why the Japanese auto industry was so vulnerable to the collapse of the American market in 2008–09. Broadly speaking, the shift of emphasis towards Asia has been the salient feature of Japanese trade in the last ten years: exports to Asia have risen from 33 to 52 per cent of the total, while exports to the United States and Europe have fallen to 17 and 13 per cent respectively. This development is due partly to the accelerating pace of Asian integration but above all to the rise of China, which became Japan's largest trading partner in 2007.

Two factors have made a particular contribution to Japan's commercial vigour: the focusing of exports on sectors of technological excellence and the power of its trading companies. The role of these *shōsha*, attached to the major *keiretsu* groups like Mitsui, Mitsubishi and Sumitomo, is dwindling as Japanese industry becomes increasingly international: they accounted for nearly 60 per cent of imports and 50 per cent of exports in 1981, compared with only 22 and 12 per cent today. The trading companies are still important players on international markets, however, since the seven-largest have over 1,000 establishments in other countries.

Free-trade agreements, especially in Asia, have helped to nourish the expansion of trade. While China pursued a strategy of active economic diplomacy, Japan lagged behind because of its reluctance to accept the agricultural component of such agreements. It is now catching up, with nineteen agreements proposed, under negotiation or concluded, compared with China's twenty-three.[27] An apparent loss of commercial power to China does not mean that Japan is less competitive, but rather that the Japanese manufacturing industry has become more international, since great swathes have relocated over the last twenty years. Offshore production has risen from 11 to 19 per cent of the total in ten years; for companies with foreign operations, the proportion has risen from 23 to 32 per cent. Thus, the export yardstick alone does not give a true reflection of Japan's global market share, which is three times larger when foreign production is included. The American market is an extreme example: only 20 per cent of "Japanese" products consumed there are imported, while 80 per cent come either from local factories or from Japanese subsidiaries located elsewhere in the world, especially Asia.[28]

The world's largest creditor nation

Japan established itself as a global financial power in the 1980s. Two main reasons explain this near sudden emergence: the real wealth generated by a highly competitive industrial sector, compounded by monetary factors which, in a huge speculative bubble, caused shares and property values to triple between 1985 and 1989.[29] The bursting of the bubble in 1990 plunged Japan into an economic crisis that lasted more than ten years.

Yet Japan remains the world's largest creditor nation because the core of its financial power was able to withstand the long period of stagnation. Household savings have been falling for a number of years but Japan still has a high gross savings ratio: 27 per cent of GDP compared with 19.3 per cent in the EU and 14 per cent in the United States. Current trade surpluses continued to accumulate even during the 1990s, and at the end of 2009 net assets held in other countries amounted to nearly USD 2.8 trillion, or 56 per cent of GDP. The income from those assets is an increasingly important item in the balance of trade and now greatly exceeds the trade surplus: Japan is still an industrious nation but it also lives on the income from its investments. Foreign assets include holdings in foreign companies, but mostly consist of financial investments, especially in US Treasuries. Japanese firms maintained their financial firepower during the crisis years and their foreign direct investment exceeds USD 500 billion, with the United States accounting for 32 per cent, Europe for 27 per cent and Asia for 24 per cent.

The financial system, on the verge of bankruptcy in 1998, has been thoroughly purged and the enormous bad debts of the 1990s, amounting to around USD 1 trillion, have been written off. Fragility persists in the insurance sector and among regional banks, but restructuring has led to the formation of three major banking groups which number among the world's largest. Although the financial crisis in 2008–09 affected the Japanese stock market, it did not threaten a banking system only marginally exposed to subprime debt; in contrast, the real economy was hit hard by the global recession. However, the financial supremacy of the world's largest creditor nation is not complete because it lacks one vital element: acceptance of the yen as a reserve currency. The yen plays a very limited role in global terms, accounting for fewer than 10 per cent of international transactions compared with 44 per cent for the dollar and 30 per cent for the euro. More surprisingly, the bulk of Japanese trade is denominated in dollars not yen: only 37 per cent of exports and 23 per cent of imports are invoiced in yen at global level and barely more in Asia. Despite an official desire to see the yen used more widely in international trade, Tokyo has been too concerned about the attendant monetary policy constraints to do very much about it.

Japan has remained a financial power throughout times of crisis and renewal but it bears the scars of the long crisis of the 1990s, in the form of a massive overhang of government debt, which in gross terms reached 200 per cent of GDP in 2010. Such debt levels are ultimately unsustainable, especially if interest rates rise, thereby increasing the debt burden and severely curtailing growth. Government debt is in effect mortgaging the country's future. Like China, Japan is a mighty but vulnerable giant, as the violent impact of a spreading global crisis has so vividly illustrated.

Considerable challenges ahead

Given their respective levels of development, the Chinese and Japanese economies will face very different challenges over the next twenty years. As a mature economy and a post-industrial society, Japan has to find new sources of growth, whereas rapid expansion is absolutely essential for China to meet the basic needs of its vast population and achieve its geopolitical ambitions.

Threats to the pace of China's expansion

The Chinese authorities are well aware of the challenges ahead. The Chinese Communist Party theorist, Zheng Bijian, explains them in terms of simple arithmetic: "All the problems are multiplied by 1.3 billion [people] and all the successes divided by the same number." The threats are both internal and external. On the domestic front, China will have to cope with a polarised society, an environmental crisis and heavy financial burdens. Other external constraints that could also slow its advance include any restriction on raw material supplies and the gradual erosion of the comparative advantages that have fuelled explosive export growth. Together, these challenges and threats could play out in such a way as to undermine the government's legitimacy, adding political uncertainty to the mix of factors liable to hinder Chinese growth.

An unequal society

Rapid growth has resulted in a spectacular reduction of poverty in China but it has also created a double rift. Social inequalities are growing and regional disparities are becoming more apparent.[30] Inequality is increasing in China, not just between cities and the countryside but also between the very poor and the new urban rich. The income gap between cities and the countryside has almost doubled in twenty years; the multiplier is now 3.5, rising to 6 if access to healthcare and education is included.[31] Rural inhabitants account for 55 per cent of China's total population, but only 11 per cent of national wealth.

In the cities, the well-off rub shoulders with the new poor: China has over 400,000 US-dollar millionaires and the income of the richest 10 per cent is ten times that of the poorest 10 per cent. These income inequalities at national level are compounded by regional disparities between the coastal provinces and the central and western provinces. Income per capita in the richest provinces is six times greater than in the poorest, whereas ten years ago it was four times. A map of regional income disparities overlaid on a map showing regional growth rates would show a high degree of congruence, since most growth centres are located in the coastal provinces. With 38 per cent of the population, they account for around 60 per cent of GDP, 90 per cent of foreign trade and, until recently, 80 per cent of foreign investment.

The government displays its intention of reducing social inequality and regional disparities in the "harmonious society" slogan, an objective proclaimed when the 11th Five-Year Plan (2006–2010) for Economic and Social Development was reaffirmed at the 17th CPC Congress in October 2007. The process of restoring a regional balance started in 2000 in the west of the country and in 2003 in the north-east. Investment in both regions has risen sharply since then, a trend that should be amplified by expansion of the high-speed rail network from 1,100 km in 2007 to 7,000 km in 2010 and 13,000 km in 2012. Central government measures to reduce the income gap were introduced in 2002 but the results to date have been disappointing and deep poverty levels have remained virtually unchanged since the late 1990s. This is due to the administrative and tax structure of such a vast country, since local governments hold sway over social policy. Growing inequality coupled with endemic corruption in local government is nourishing deep-seated frustration among those left behind in the dash for growth, often culminating in "public order disturbances" or "large-scale incidents."[32] Most of these popular revolts have their roots in similar grievances. In the countryside, the cause is generally expropriation at derisory prices; in the cities, unpaid wages or redundancy terms, especially in State enterprises, which have laid off tens of millions of workers since the mid-1990s. Being specific by nature, these actions have been limited in scope and have not led to large-scale civil unrest at regional or national level. However, the number of incidents is rising: 87,000 in 2006, according to the latest official statistics, ten times more than in 1993. The social divide is a source of instability that the government views with great concern, knowing that the social cohesion necessary for strong growth would be threatened should the rift continue to widen.

Warding off ecological disaster

The second threat to the future pace of growth is the disastrous ecological impact of untrammelled industrialisation and rapid urbanisation. With coal supplying 64 per cent of its primary energy needs, China overtook the United States as the world's biggest emitter of carbon dioxide in 2007, generating 21 per cent of the world total.[33] More than a third of river water is unfit for any type of use, half the aquifers are polluted and 300 million country-dwellers drink non-drinkable water. Energy consumption more than doubled between 2000 and 2008; and, despite the progress made since the 1980s, energy efficiency is still ten times lower than in Japan. The situation is all the more worrying given that China's demand for energy, now 15 per cent of the world total, is likely to almost double by 2030 and coal will meet 60 per cent of the increased needs. But the worst may be yet to come. The vice minister for the environment, Pan Yue, made no bones about the matter in 2005:[34] "In the future we will have [...] over 150 million migrants for ecological reasons or, if you prefer, environmental refugees." The damage in public health terms is devastating[35] but the financial cost is also very high, between 3 and 6 per cent of annual GDP according to a World Bank study.[36] Ecological impacts are also a contributory factor to civil unrest and protests against pollution from nearby factories are increasing: between 2001 and 2005, for example, authorities depending on the Environment Ministry (SEPA) received over 2.5 million letters and 430,000 visits from 597,000 petitioners.[37]

The necessary laws and regulations are in place and over a third of the 2009–10 stimulus plan is devoted to "green" growth. But as with reducing inequality, Beijing's objectives are not necessarily those of the provinces, most of which are more interested in going for growth. This tension between the centre and the periphery is a manifestation of the "fragmented author-itarianism" of the Chinese regime, whose contradictions arise from internal clashes between rival bureaucratic factions.[38] A more balanced distribution of powers between central and provincial government would be necessary to ensure contin-ued growth at a perhaps slower but ultimately more sustaina-ble pace.

If that were the case much of the environmental damage could probably be reversed, as the Japanese example has shown. Pol-lution in China today resembles the pollution in Japan in the 1960s, when steel mills and chemical plants poured gases and effluent into the atmosphere, the rivers and the sea. From the mid-1970s, two factors helped to initiate a genuine ecological revolution: popular protest and, above all, the oil shock, which forced Japan to change its production methods. The country became an exemplar of environmental protection and its indus-tries developed highly effective energy-saving technologies. If there is one area in which cooperation between China and Japan could prove especially fruitful it is there. According to a recent McKinsey study,[39] China's annual CO_2 emissions will double by

2030 unless drastic measures are taken, whereas they could be held at close to the present level by using currently available technologies. Japan could enable China to benefit from these, always supposing China was willing to let foreign firms into its vast green technologies market, estimated to be worth over USD 500 billion by 2013.[40]

At UN climate change conferences in 2009, China stated that it would increase the proportion of renewable sources in its energy consumption by 15–20 per cent by 2020. It also proposed to reduce the carbon intensity of its economy by about 40 per cent, or even 45 per cent, in relation to 2005 levels.[41] The minimum agreement, which was concluded on 19 December 2009 under questionable conditions at the disastrous Copenhagen climate change summit, underlined not only the north-south divide but also, and above all, the irreconcilable positions of China and the United States. The US, which has not ratified the Kyoto Protocol, proposed to reduce its CO_2 emissions by 17 per cent by 2020 in relation to 2005, giving a very modest 4 per cent reduction in relation to 1990 levels.[42] And conditions were attached to even this paltry effort: the emerging countries, with China foremost among them, would have to take equivalent measures and submit to independent external verification. The demands were unacceptable to Beijing and progress made at the subsequent Cancun conference in December 2010 was not very significant in this respect. As it stands,[43] the Copenhagen Accord merely contains non-binding declarations of intent, in contrast to the Kyoto Protocol, which expires in 2012. In all events, the lesson to be learnt from Copenhagen seems unambiguous: it is not pressure from the developed world, and especially the United States, that will make China do more to protect the environment, but pressure from Chinese public opinion and the choices that Beijing will have to make between the pace and the quality of growth.

China's financial burdens

Financial constraints could also hold back growth, because the cost of providing comprehensive social protection (the system is still very fragmented) and supporting a fragile banking system could be very high.

The ending of people's communes and swingeing job cuts in State-owned industry led to the gradual disappearance of the "iron rice bowl," which provided the workers in the system with lifetime employment, medical care and a pension. Among urban workers, it is estimated that 45 per cent have a basic pension entitlement, 40 per cent have unemployment insurance and only around 30 per cent have health insurance. In the countryside, only 20 per cent of an estimated rural population of 750 million have health cover. A step towards comprehensive social protection, especially health insurance, was taken in the stimulus plan introduced in October 2008. Although it will impose a huge burden on the public purse, it is unavoidable if the government wants to achieve its goal of a "moderately well-off society" and ensure long-term social stability. The aim is to have a universal basic system in place by 2020, at a total cost of 5.74 trillion yuan (USD 850 billion), with 24 per cent being earmarked for pensions, 18 per cent for health insurance and 34 per cent for education.[44] The financial cost of such a system is likely to become increasingly onerous, and perhaps even crushing, as the population ages and the labour force shrinks, which it will from 2015–20. Although China is currently better placed than Japan in that respect, it will have a rapidly ageing population from 2015. From 6.8 per cent in 2000, over-65s are expected to represent 12 per cent of the population in 2020 and 16 per cent in 2030. The number of workers per retiree will fall from its current level of nine to four by 2030.[45] In short, China could well find itself "old before it gets rich."

Support for a fragile and inefficient banking sector constitutes another foreseeable financial burden. Since the 1995 banking reform, four large State banks have dominated the industry, taking more than half of all deposits. They have excellent liquidity, since loans represent only 75 per cent of deposits, but remain fragile from a solvency standpoint. Still bearing the imprint of the previous system, they lend mainly to State companies of very disparate quality in terms of profitability and solvency. Subject to political pressures and lacking effective risk management, they accumulated a vast stock of bad debt in the 1990s which amounted to USD 400 billion in 2000, or 36 per cent of their total lending. Since then, these bad debts have been transferred to special-purpose public companies, so the State will have to assume the residual cost. The bad debt ratio had fallen to just 1.7 per cent by September 2009 but there is a risk that bank lending to companies weakened by the crisis of 2008–09 will lead to further write-offs. In budgetary terms China's current situation is relatively sound: even after the massive two-year stimulus plan, the deficit does not exceed 3 per cent of GDP. Public debt, at around 20 per cent of GDP, is at an enviable level, but if pension commitments and guarantees extended to public bodies are included that figure rises to 60 per cent and perhaps even higher. Although China has substantial foreign currency reserves it has limited scope for significantly greater budget expenditure on social welfare and the banking sector, all the more so as the Chinese government bond market is underdeveloped and lacking liquidity when compared to Japan.

Hungry for raw materials

Another factor holding back rapid medium-term growth is China's dependence on other countries for supplies of raw materials. China, unlike Japan, has substantial mineral resources—coal, oil, metals, etc.—but it also has 20 per cent of the world's population on 7 per cent of its landmass. In relation to 1.3 billion inhabitants, those resources are insufficient to fuel very rapid and, it must be said, highly profligate growth.

The world's leading producer of coal, iron ore, lead, tin, mercury and rare metals, China is also in second or third place for many other minerals. However, the explosion of industrial demand has resulted in a massive influx of imports, worth USD 60 billion a year net, plus USD 100 billion of oil products. The pressure of Chinese demand, sustained by exceptional financial resources, goes a long way to explaining the surge in raw material prices since 2005. China accounts for between 20 and 35 per cent of world demand, depending on the minerals concerned, whereas value-added industry represents only 12 per cent of the total. It also has enormous energy needs: it already uses 17.7 per cent of the world's primary energy output and that proportion is likely to double by 2030. The main energy sources are coal (64 per cent) and oil (18 per cent). Despite being the world's leading hydropower generator with 15 per cent of the total, the proliferation of nuclear power stations and a growing contribution from renewable energy sources,[46] the proportion of coal in the energy mix will fall only slightly by 2030, causing CO_2 emissions to double. Coal is the only energy source in which China, the world's largest producer with 47 per cent of the total, is self-sufficient. In contrast, it is becoming increasingly dependent on oil, of which it is the world's second-largest consumer after the United States. Self-sufficient until 1992, it now imports more than half of its consumption requirement, making it the world's second-largest importer behind the United States and ahead of Japan.[47] China's imports are likely to triple by 2030 and its oil dependency rate could rise to 80 per cent, considering that the number of cars in the country is expected to increase fivefold to 270 million. Saudi Arabia, Iran and Angola are its biggest suppliers at present, but in order to meet its future needs it has invested over USD 40 billion in twenty or so countries in Latin America, Africa and Central and South-East Asia.[48] However, that will not reduce the predominant role in China's oil supply played by the Middle East, whose contribution is likely to rise to 70 per cent in 2015 compared with 58 per cent now.

In order to reduce its dependence on other countries for raw materials and energy, China is intensifying the search for new reserves at home (including offshore). Explorations in Tibet have been promising: the government's intransigence on the Tibet issue is due not only to an obsession with territorial integrity but also to the province's wealth of mineral resources. As well as copper, iron, zinc and lead, they also include lithium, essential for rechargeable batteries and hence for the production of electric cars, a sector in which China has great ambitions. Nonetheless, most new resources will come from abroad, and the concern to secure supplies defines the geographical outlines of a highly active economic diplomacy. Given the predicted end of conventional oil extraction by 2050 and the gradual depletion of planetary reserves of certain minerals, the risk of a severe curb on industrial expansion worldwide is real indeed. There is an abundance of hydrocarbon and mineral wealth in the Arctic but exploiting it would create an ecological disaster. If further reserves are not found elsewhere or if the undersea mining of polymetallic nodules proves impractical or prohibitively expensive, these limits are likely to curb industrial growth throughout the world, and particularly in China.

The erosion of China's comparative advantages

The unstoppable expansion of China's trade has been founded on low labour costs, a major advantage that has had an important structural effect on China's place in global commerce. An undervalued currency has also helped to swell its trade surpluses. Can these two key elements of Chinese competitiveness last?

Low wages and scant social security provision mean that labour costs in China are about twenty times lower than in developed countries. Those costs are likely to soar over the next ten years as a result of substantial wage rises, comparable to those seen between 2001 and 2007 (15 per cent a year on average), the introduction of a statutory minimum wage in 2008 and higher social security charges to fund universal health and pension cover. Pressure for considerably higher wages may be expected to spread following the strikes that hit Honda and Foxcom factories in June 2010. However, the increases are not likely to compromise China's international competitiveness: productivity gains will make up for much of the additional outlay and there will still be an enormous margin in relation to labour costs in the United States, Japan and Europe. It looks as though that particular comparative advantage will last for some time yet, continuing to give Chinese industry a formidable competitive edge.

As for undervaluation, an undervalued currency makes Chinese products more competitive, but seen from the United States and Europe it constitutes an unfair advantage.[49] The situation is highly reminiscent of the early 1980s, when the United States blamed its soaring trade deficits with Japan on an undervalued yen. Is the yuan ridiculously undervalued? And would revaluation correct trade imbalances? It is difficult to answer the first question as China's currency is not fully convertible and estimates of an unmanaged equilibrium rate vary widely.[50] However, it is certain that runaway current account surpluses would have caused the yuan to appreciate much more since 2005 if it had been allowed to float freely. So we can assume that it remains undervalued, probably by 20 to 30 per cent, depending on the counterpart currency, dollar or euro.[51] Would a revaluation on that scale reduce American and European trade deficits? Most probably to begin with, though by less than some might hope: a 25 per cent revaluation would reduce the United States' bilateral deficit with China by only 20 per cent and its overall trade deficit by only 5 per cent. The yuan appreciated by over 20 per cent against the dollar between July 2005 and July 2008 but that did not stop the US trade deficit from continuing to soar.

Japan's experience in the 1980s is instructive from this standpoint because the almost doubling in value of the yen against the dollar between 1985 and 1987 did not put an end to the US trade deficit with Japan. The main cause was not an undervalued yen but the technological competitiveness of Japanese products. The competitiveness of Chinese products is based primarily on low labour costs and hence their price in yuan. An undervalued currency merely makes them more price-competitive. Reflecting the regional division of labour, most of the trade deficits with China are simply transfers of previous American and European deficits with other Asian countries, especially Japan. It is true that China represented 67 per cent of the US deficit with Asia in 2008, compared with 13 per cent in 1990, but it is often overlooked that Asia's share of the total US deficit fell from 64 to 48 per cent over the same period.[52]

Nevertheless, the appreciation of the yuan is far too small in view of a current account surplus of 6 per cent of GDP in 2009 and as much as 10 per cent before the crisis. Surpluses on that scale are a dangerous anomaly for a developing country, even if China regards them as a form of self-protection against possible financial crises generated by global imbalances. The government froze the yuan-dollar parity at the start of the global financial crisis to limit the deterioration of foreign trade, but that also means that China's central bank has had to reflect very low US interest rates. There is a real risk of creating a vast monetary bubble, as happened in Japan, but its bursting would have more serious consequences since the shock wave would hit Asia first, and then the rest of the world, because of China's central role in global production and trade flows. If it had been maintained, the de facto pegging of the yuan to an excessively weak dollar—i.e. of the currency of the economy with the biggest surplus to that of the economy with the biggest deficit—would have represented a serious threat to international financial stability. Having understood that such a development would not be in their interest, the

Chinese authorities decided on 19 June 2010 to manage their currency more flexibly. As they did between 2005 and 2008, they will control the extent to which the yuan is allowed to float, but it will be pegged to a basket of currencies and not just the dollar. So it is to be hoped that the world's emergence from crisis will be accompanied by a gradual but sustained appreciation of the yuan.[53] We may therefore conclude that this comparative advantage will likely be eroded to the point of extinction, unlike the labour cost advantage, which will remain the foundation of China's competitiveness.

China's political trade-off

Since the 1980s, the Communist Party's legitimacy has been based not on the Chinese people's belief in its ideology but on an economic policy that has increased everyone's purchasing power, albeit unequally. Internal challenges and external constraints will dampen the pace of growth, even after the world has emerged from recession. What would happen if growth levels were to fall over a long period? Social unrest would spread, but it would be unlikely to spark off a mass movement that could threaten the regime. Of course we should not forget the events of Tiananmen Square, for they took place at a time when the economic situation had deteriorated, but the movement calling for a "fifth modernisation" (multiparty democracy) was primarily political.[54] However, the fear of major social disturbance is still very much an issue for China's leadership and is likely to accelerate the adjustment of economic policy. The Central Committee is split between advocates of very rapid growth, whatever the social and environmental cost, and those who would like to see fairer and more sustainable development. Against the background of economic crisis, slower growth and climate change negotiations, it is possible that the latter may have gained the upper hand. To take up Benoît Vermander's enlightening distinction between "brown China" and "green China,"[55] current developments are likely to reinforce the "green" paradigm. The obsession with economic power, even at the price of heavy-handed social control and wasted resources, will doubtless gradually give way to policies more concerned with the reduction of inequalities, protection of the environment and the fight against corruption. Such a move would have a dual advantage for China's authoritarian regime: as well as winning wider popular support, the shift in emphasis to the domestic market would reduce the country's excessive reliance on international demand, the dangers of which were revealed by the crisis.

The CPC leadership does not appear to be in danger if it puts an end to the most egregious disorders that the huge changes of the last twenty years have created. As Jean-Luc Domenach has pointed out, "Since their survival has been assured and hope has entered their lives, the population has become indifferent to politics."[56] A better standard of living remains the only criterion for gaining popular support, even if there is little indulgence in attitudes towards a hierarchy all too often corrupt.[57] Within the CPC itself, the ideas of consultation and democratisation promoted by Jiang Zemin[58] have fizzled out. At the Central Committee meeting in September 2009, President Hu Jintao paid lip-service to his predecessor's slogan "Inner-party democracy is the life of the party," but immediately added "Centralism and unity are the guarantee of its strength." The government has already embarked on the intricate process of selecting those who will assume the top positions in 2012, but it takes place under a cloak of secrecy.[59] No relaxation is to be expected at present in the political sphere, where the CPC maintains strict social control in order to suppress any move towards democratisation, immediately denounced as a "subversion of State power." That was the justification for the draconian sentence imposed in December 2009 on the dissident Liu Xiaobo, co-author of the pro-democracy manifesto, Charter 08.

In a quite different sphere, mounting separatist sentiment in China's outer reaches also looks unlikely to threaten the regime's stability. The response to events in Tibet in 2008 and Xinqiang in 2009 was unequivocal: territorial integrity is an overriding obsession for the government, whose inflexible stance enjoys broad public support.

A bleak outlook for Japanese growth

Japan was the OECD country hardest hit by the crisis, experiencing the worst recession in its history during 2009. Compounding the violence of the shock caused by the collapse of global demand, the Japanese economy has structural weaknesses that will sap its future performance. Compared with China's potential, the prospects for long-term growth are poor. Productivity gains decelerate in an economy that has reached Japan's stage of maturity: markets for many products are saturated and domestic demand is small in comparison with other regional or continental economies, like those of India and China. Four other factors also cloud Japan's economic horizon: its demographics, its public sector debt, its reliance on others for its energy supply and its chronic political inertia.

Japan's demographic challenge

Demographic decline, aggravated by a rapidly ageing population, is the most serious of these handicaps since it is irreversible. It results from a scissor-effect that produces an ever-widening gap between low birth rates and rising life expectancy. The Japanese have few children: 1.37 per woman, compared with 2.02 in France and 1.65 in the OECD countries as a whole. They also have the world's greatest life expectancy: eighty-two years on average, compared with seventy-four in Europe and seventy-seven in the United States. While such longevity is to be welcomed, the low birth rate is rather perplexing. Although it can be explained to some extent by the lack of space in urban dwellings and insufficient childcare provision, it is possible that the reluctance to have children reflects a lack of confidence in the future. Under the dual effect of a low birth rate and a cultural aversion to immigration, the total population has begun to shrink. After peaking at 128 million in 2004, it is likely to fall to 117 million in 2030 and 102 million in 2050. The decline in the labour force, which has already begun, will be even more spectacular, as the working-age population is projected to fall from 82 million in 2010 to 69 million in 2030 and 52 million in 2050.

Uniquely in the world, Japan has not only a shrinking population but also a rapidly ageing one, since the proportion of older people rose from 7 per cent in 1970 to 23 per cent in 2008. Given the large number of baby-boomers, the over-65s are likely to account for 31 per cent of the population in 2030 and 38 per cent in 2050.[60]

Demographic effects and a greying population will weigh heavily on the pace of growth. The reduction in the working-age population—13 million fewer by 2030—will have a direct impact on production capacity. Potential growth could be cut by more than half a percentage point over the next two decades to barely 1.5 per cent a year including productivity gains.[61] An ageing population will also inevitably cost more in healthcare and pensions, which will have to be funded from a shrinking base.

The government has not just sat on its hands, but the scale of the challenge warrants much greater political determination. Countering the decline in the labour force would require positive incentives for prospective parents and mass immigration in a country where foreigners account for only 1.6 per cent of the total population. The few measures taken in recent years to encourage families to have more children, such as parental leave and more day nurseries, are on too small a scale, while the government does not dare tackle the powerful cultural aversion to immigration in Japanese society.

To make up for a shrinking labour force, government policy seeks above all to exploit two potential resources: older people working beyond retirement age and women, whose employment rate is lower than in other countries. Over half of Japanese women leave the workplace when they have their first child and do not return until roughly twenty years later. If their employment rate was the same as that of men, the labour force could be maintained at its current level. In contrast, there is less scope to limit the impact of an ageing population on welfare budgets. Pension and health insurance schemes have had to be reformed several times so that they remain financially balanced and sustainable, through measures such as rising the retirement age, increasing contributions and reducing benefits.

However, although an ageing population is a major handicap, it does have some positive aspects. The first relates to consumption, because older Japanese people feel liberated from the self-imposed frugality of supportive parenting. The second concerns research and development, because a shrinking labour force and the healthcare needs of an ageing population stimulate research in areas such as robotics and domestic automation. Through progress in tackling age-related problems, Japan will be able to offer innovative products and services, for which global demand will soar in the coming decades.

Nonetheless, the irreversible decline of the labour force poses a long-term threat to Japan's economic power and hence to its clout in Asia. Yet a solution could be found within the broader region, which has an abundance of skilled labour. The encouragement of immigration from other Asian countries would serve a dual purpose for Japan, since it would preserve its growth potential while increasing its influence in the regionalisation process, hitherto limited to the liberalisation of trade and investment. The example of India stands out in this respect. At a time when Tokyo is negotiating a strategic partnership with New Delhi to contain Chinese ambitions, its proposals for opening the Japanese labour market to Indian engineers and technicians have been regrettably feeble. The cultural aversion to immigration is plainly still very strong and it is symptomatic that the new governing party should have so little to say on the subject, preferring to advance pro-child policies that present less of an electoral minefield. Yet greater openness to immigration from Asia would enable Japan not only to preserve its economic vitality but also to enhance its role and image in the region.

Japan's public sector debt

The fallout from the demographic time-bomb will be all the more difficult to absorb given that Japan's public finances are already in a parlous state. With gross public sector debt approaching 200 per cent of GDP in 2010, compared with 173 per cent in 2008, Japan holds the OECD record. It is true that, unlike in the United States and Europe, almost all the debt is financed by domestic investors, for the time being at very low interest rates. It is also true that net public sector debt—about 107 per cent of GDP after stripping out holdings of financial assets—is more reasonable, but the trend since 1995 has been alarming in both gross and net terms, since gross debt has doubled and net debt has tripled. Much of the massive debt overhang is attributable to the numerous stimulus plans introduced during the crisis of the 1990s, costing a total of USD 1 trillion. The Koizumi government (2001–06) kept the lid on debt and slashed the public sector deficit from 8.2 per cent of GDP in 2002 to 3.3 per cent in 2006. However, the overall fiscal deficit rose again to 5.4 per cent in 2008 and jumped to 11.4 per cent in 2009 in response to a combination of stimulus plans and falling tax revenue. Estimated at 9.6 per cent in 2010, it was projected to narrow somewhat to 8.9 per cent in 2011,[62] but that seems out of reach after the triple disaster which hit the north-east of Japan on 11 March 2011.

In addition to economic factors linked to a succession of crises, government debt has been swollen by a structural imbalance in the public finances. The new Democratic Party of Japan (DPJ) majority wants to cut spending but most of it can hardly be reduced, given that welfare budgets are bound to rise and government is already very lean (the public sector accounts for only 5 per cent of jobs, compared with 22 per cent in France).[63] The problem lies on the revenue side. Most revenue stems from direct taxes but the tax base is small and subject to the vicissitudes of the economic cycle, whereas consumption tax (Japan's version of VAT) is only 5 per cent. To reduce the budget deficit the rate of this very broad tax will have to be increased but any reform is bound to be gradual. Politicians are extremely reluctant to introduce a highly unpopular measure that would also depress consumption and growth, at least in the short-term. The DPJ's rise to power further complicates the tax equation, since the announced budget cuts will doubtless not be sufficient to fund its ambitious programme of welfare spending and consumption-led recovery. Its defeat in the Upper House elections in July 2010 was due in large measure to the prospect of an increase in consumption tax mentioned by prime minister Naoto Kan.

Japan's soaring public sector debt raises two questions: how can it be refinanced, and how can interest payments be met? On the first point, Japan is in a position diametrically opposed to that of the United States, even though US debt is proportionately smaller. The United States has to fund half of its public sector deficit by selling debt to other countries. Japan, on the other hand, has substantial foreign currency reserves and a savings surplus: 93 per cent of its debt is taken up by its own citizens. So unlike the United States, Japan's high level of government debt does not leave it dependent on other countries. However, Japan will have to rely more heavily on foreign investors in a few years' time, given the trend decline in the household savings ratio from 10 per cent of disposable income in 1999 to 3.3 per cent in 2009. What about interest payments, which already represent 23 per cent of the budget? Japan has benefited from many years of very low interest rates, but a sharp rise, though unlikely in the short-term, would have a devastating effect. It is the sword of Damocles hanging over Japanese growth, for it will take many years to defuse the time-bomb of massive government debt. Without vigorous corrective measures, gross public sector debt could reach 250 per cent of GDP in 2015.

Japan's dependence on imported energy and raw materials

Japan is almost entirely dependent on other countries to satisfy its energy and raw material needs, but its economy is very energy-efficient and manufacturing industry is less prevalent than in China. With comparable GDP, Japan consumes 4.7 per cent of world energy against China's 15 per cent. There is also a marked difference between them in terms of primary energy sources: gas and oil account for 35 per cent of Japan's energy needs, nuclear power for about a quarter, coal for another quarter and renewables for the remaining 15 per cent.[64] Japan's sources of supply for natural gas and coal are relatively diversified but it gets 90 per cent of its oil from the Middle East, thereby creating a major vulnerability which will increase as the country will have to import more fossil fuels after the closure of the Fukushima nuclear plant and probably several others in similar locations. Its energy policy over the past decades has been based on three interwoven strands: energy savings, sustainable development and diversification of supply.

Japan's experience in energy saving goes back to the first oil shock of 1973; since then it has become 40 per cent more energy-efficient. Japanese firms have constantly refined their production methods in response to that imperative, developing innovative technologies to make optimum use of energy. It is the world leader in energy efficiency, with a coefficient of 0.10,[65] ahead of Europe (0.19), the United States (0.21) and China (0.90). The 2006 New National Strategy for Energy calls for a further 30 per cent improvement by 2030. The constant quest for energy efficiency is coupled with ambitious environmental protection goals, especially against the greenhouse effect. The world's second-largest economy until 2009, Japan is only the fifth-largest emitter of CO_2 with 4 per cent of the total, well behind China (21 per cent) and the United States (20 per cent). It is the only Asian country bound by the Kyoto Protocol. Although Japan has fallen behind in relation to its target of a 6 per cent reduction in emissions by 2012 in relation to 1990, the ruling DPJ aims to go much further and has set a target of 25 per cent in 2020 in relation to 1990. Energy efficiency and environmental concerns thus drive a proactive policy of diversifying energy resources, the structure of which will ultimately have to change profoundly. In the meantime, Japan engages in active economic diplomacy to diversify its sources of supply, especially in Russia and Central Asia (and in consequence often finds itself in competition with China). However, Japan's reliance on Middle East oil will be mitigated only very slowly. Consequently there are two deviations from its general alignment with American foreign policy: it is relatively pro-Arab in its stance on the conflict between Israel and Palestine and, at the risk of incurring Washington's displeasure, it maintains "friendly" ties and close links with Iran, its third-largest oil supplier (and also an important supplier to China).

The end of political paralysis in sight?

The Japanese elections on 30 August 2009 have been described as a "political earthquake." After more than half a century of conservative rule, the centre-left DPJ won a crushing victory over the Liberal Democratic Party (LDP), a coalition of disparate factions ranging from the nationalist right to the centre-right. A historical turning point, the elections put an end to the political stalemate that had afflicted Japan since the crisis of the 1990s and been the major obstacle preventing a return to long-term growth. Until the late 1980s, Japan's success was based on a national resolve that channelled its energies first into rebuilding the country, and then into catching up with the United States. In the "LDP" or "1955" system, the LDP dominated the political arena and formed governments but the real power lay elsewhere, in the hands of the "iron triangle," in which politicians, technocrats and business leaders were closely involved in framing an economic policy based on their community of interests. Although their hegemony was occasionally eclipsed, this motley crew had been constantly in power since 1955, except for a brief parenthesis in 1993–94.

In the 1990s, the financial crisis and the effects of globalisation shook the power structure. Mistrust of the elite spread and low turnouts at elections reflected civil society's disaffection with a political machine widely regarded as corrupted, pandering to special interests, paralysed by factional infighting and incapable of implementing a coherent programme of reform. Ten prime ministers came and went during a decade of crisis, which affected not only the economy but also society as a whole.

In this context of political stalemate, Junichiro Koizumi's accession of power in April 2001 came as a surprise and a ray of hope. The key elements of his neo-liberal reforms were decentralisation and privatisation, policies that he resolutely implemented. He strengthened the role of the executive and tried to put an end to factional infighting; at the same time the rise of the DPJ, born from dissenting factions within the LDP, held out the hope of a real democratic alternative. By the end of Koizumi's term in 2006, Japan seemed to have come to grips with the new challenges posed by globalisation and to have embarked on a genuine modernisation of its political and socio-economic structures. But the old guard soon regained the upper hand, instability returned and three more prime ministers came and went before the elections of 30 August 2009.

The crushing victory of the DPJ led by Yukio Hatoyama owed more to massive rejection of the LDP than to genuine endorsement of the DPJ manifesto, centred on two essential aims: to return the power previously usurped by the civil service to the executive and parliament, and to create a more fraternal and egalitarian society. The economic programme was a sort of revolution. For the first time, the proposed model focused on household demand, not investment and exports, while measures to encourage families to have more children sought to halt the demographic decline. The new government offered a boost to purchasing power and support for small businesses, farmers, the unemployed and families with children in a new policy designed to espouse individual aspirations. Directed more towards the losers from globalisation than the winners and promising them better social protection, it was clearly intended to signal a break from the market-oriented policies of LDP governments. Denouncing "US-led globalism" and the "dictatorship of the market," Hatoyama promoted a model of society along European lines and a more independent foreign policy in relation to the United States. He believed that Japan, as a regional power, should strengthen its ties with Asia, and especially with China. The electorate was not expecting miracles, having been let down all too often in the past, and wondered how such a costly programme was to be funded. Giving them good reason to be cautious, the new government got off to a laboured start, to say the least. Hampered by difficulties in getting ministries to cooperate, the latent hostility of big business, the ditching of certain campaign promises, the revelation of party funding scandals, the finance minister's resignation and, above all, concerns about Hatoyama's abilities, its popularity rating fell by more than twenty points in four months. The honeymoon period ended on 24 December 2009 when Hatoyama had to apologise on television for his party's funding irregularities. His disastrous handling of the issue of the American military base at Futenma on Okinawa and his lack of leadership culminated in his resignation and replacement by Naoto Kan in June 2010. Does this mark a "new beginning," as Kan has claimed, or a return to political instability?

After the Upper House elections in July 2010 and the infighting within the DPJ which followed, it is difficult to give an answer. If the DPJ had been successful, it would have spelt the end of the "1955 system" and its replacement by a kind of "2009 system," a reshaping of the political landscape based on alternation. As it is, the DPJ's defeat may raise fears of the formation of ragbag coalitions that will limit the government's room for manoeuvre. But however that may be, a sea-change occurred in September 2009: by issuing their rebuff at the polls, the Japanese showed that they were not resigned to the political inertia which, apart from the Koizumi interlude, had paralysed the country for twenty years or more. Perhaps it can be seen as another instance of Japan's capacity to bounce back from the many crises it has experienced.

Giants shaken by the crisis

Until the crisis struck, the idea that Asia might be economically decoupled from the rest of the world had steadily gained credibility, despite the apparent contradiction with the very concept of a globalised economy. The argument was that the expansion of domestic markets and regional integration had combined to enable independent growth in Asia. Global recession seemed to put an end to that theory, but the complexity of the crisis, initially financial then economic, calls for a more detailed analysis.

The financial crisis hit Chinese and Japanese stock markets hard but did not spread to banking systems in Asia. Subprime contagion stopped at the doors of Japan and China[66] because the 1990s crisis had made Japanese banks risk-averse, and because China has a banking system with strict capital controls and relatively little international exposure. Japanese and Chinese banks have remained highly liquid thanks to abundant domestic savings, much of it in the form of bank deposits. China and Japan did not therefore suffer the dual solvency and liquidity crisis that hit Western banks. The financial crisis did not really affect Asia and from that standpoint talk of decoupling is indeed justified.

That is not at all the case in the real economy. The crisis spread through foreign trade channels and domestic markets were not sufficiently robust to withstand the effects of a slump in global demand. China's economy grew by 13 per cent in 2007 but only 9.6 per cent in 2008, its lowest level in seven years. Although domestic demand has held up well thanks to internal investment, exports to recession-hit developed nations have fallen sharply. That explains the significant slowdown in growth, which has led to a sharp rise in unemployment, especially among internal migrant workers, some 20 million of whom (about 15 per cent of the total) have been laid off. The Chinese government started looking at worst-case scenarios as soon as the crisis began, including the risk of serious civil unrest that would be difficult to control if growth fell below 5–6 per cent. That is why, in November 2008, the government introduced a huge two-year stimulus plan worth 15 per cent of GDP, or almost USD 600 billion. The plan gave priority to investment, especially in infrastructure and environmental projects, but also included measures to promote rural development, expand welfare provision and support innovation, while a relaxed monetary stance helped business investment. Growth reached 9.2 per cent in 2009 and 10.3 per cent in 2010. Yet this unexpected achievement should not mask the true state of affairs. The surge in bank lending has exacerbated industrial overcapacity[67] and may fuel a property and stock market bubble, the bursting of which would leave a massive overhang of bad debt. Even more worrying, the stimulus plan has worsened rather than improved the quality of growth. Investment has taken over from faltering external demand and was responsible for over 90 per cent of growth in 2009. Continuing in 2010, the stimulus plan did little to redirect the Chinese economy towards stronger domestic demand. Consumption as a proportion of GDP fell from 47 per cent in 1996 to 37 per cent in 2008 while exports jumped from 20 to 35 per cent. There are two reasons for the decline: household income has fallen sharply as a proportion of national wealth (from 70 to 55 per cent) and the lack of a broad-based welfare system has encouraged a high level of precautionary savings. Refocusing on the domestic market would therefore require a rise in household income (wages and social transfers) and much more extensive welfare provision. This change in the growth model is a vital necessity, for the crisis has highlighted China's excessive dependence on export markets. This also holds true for Japan, which, for the same reason, has experienced the worst recession in its history.

Japanese growth turned negative in the spring of 2008, even before the financial crisis reached its peak. The economy had grown steadily since 2002, though exports accounted for 60 per cent of the growth while domestic consumption remained sluggish in a deflationary environment. That six-year cycle, one of the longest in the post-war period, came to an abrupt end in the second quarter of 2008 with the slowing of global growth. The second half of 2008 was disastrous. The combined effects of global recession and a sharp rise in the value of the yen (23 per cent against the euro and 20 per cent against the dollar in 2008) caused a collapse in exports to the United States, its largest market (20 per cent), and Europe, its third-largest market

(15 per cent), especially in high-tech sectors like automobiles and electronics.

Paradoxically, it is the steady rise in the technology content of exports—an index of 130 in 2009 from a baseline 100 in 2000[68]—that explains why Japan was hit so hard. Its domination of high-end segments proved counter-productive when export markets for such items collapsed. China suffered less because, with the exception of electronic goods, it mostly exports low value-added products. Textiles are its biggest export sector to the United States, accounting for about 35 per cent of the total, whereas for Japan it is high-end automobiles (45 per cent). The contraction of world trade caused a fall in Japanese exports and hence in business investment, while rising unemployment and falling wages stifled household consumption. In 2009, with GDP shrinking by 5 per cent and unemployment running at record levels, Japan experienced its worst post-war recession and the most severe of all the industrialised nations. Growth in 2010 reached 3.9 per cent but this exceptional performance was due to temporary stimulus measures. Before the catastrophe of March 2011, growth for 2011 and following years was projected to range between 1.5 and 2.4 per cent, provided that there was a vigorous international recovery, especially in China, which accounts for nearly 20 per cent of Japanese exports. But a further slide was not ruled out, as Japan's emergence from the crisis is handicapped by the return of deflationary pressures and the sharp appreciation of the yen against the dollar.[69] The triple disaster that has hit the country will obviously have a deep impact on economic growth, which could be negative in 2011 and then resume in 2012 if the situation at the Fukushima nuclear plant is stabilised.

To face the global crisis, the new Hatoyama government announced a fresh stimulus package on 7 December 2009, following on from the four previous plans launched between October 2008 and May 2009. Altogether, these plans have amounted to over 6 per cent of GDP, which will further increase the debt burden.[70] The government was already finding it hard to finance manifesto promises,[71] but that will be far more difficult, or even impossible, as reconstruction costs in the devastated regions alone may reach 5 to 6 per cent of GDP.

Two lessons may be learned from the crisis. First, the growth gap between China and Japan is widening, the latter's structural problems having been thrown into stark relief by the crisis. Second, Asia's economic decoupling is largely illusory because stronger and faster recovery owes much to the scale of stimulus plans, the effects of which will be short-lived. The entire region still needs to focus on growth driven by domestic consumption. China is over-reliant on export demand, especially from the United States and Europe. It would have to reduce the contribution of net exports to growth by developing its domestic market, while also adjusting the mix of its export destinations by increasing the respective shares of Latin America, Russia, the Middle East and Africa. The crisis could ultimately prove beneficial for China, giving impetus to a redefinition of its economic model. Nothing could be less certain, however, because that would mean initially trimming one or two points off growth until domestic demand could take up the slack left by reduced external demand caused by appreciation of the yuan. China argues that there is no need to allow its currency to rise because the global slowdown has automatically reduced exports and the stimulus plan encourages imports. It is true that the current account surplus fell to 6 per cent of GDP in 2009 compared with 10.6 and 9.6 per cent in 2007 and 2008 respectively, and that IMF forecasts in October 2010 suggest that it will remain between 5 and 7 per cent over the next few years. However, that is still excessive for an emerging country and points to an imbalance in the drivers of growth.

For Japan, the crisis exposes the limits of the 2002–07 growth cycle.[72] Until the crisis of the 1990s, the challenges lay on the supply side: the imperative was to develop production capacity and increase productivity gains. Since then the balance has shifted to the demand side: insufficient household consumption was offset by public sector investment during the 1990s, then by external demand from 2002. The 2002–7 cycle helped to eliminate previous excesses—debt and overcapacity—but failed to invigorate low private consumption, a structural weakness of the Japanese economy. Exports took over, accounting for 60 per cent of growth: they represented 17.5 per cent of GDP in 2007 (and 16 per cent in 2008), compared with only 11 per cent in 2002. If Japan wants to stay on the path of sustainable growth and become less vulnerable to international economic circumstances, it urgently needs to adjust its model. The changes advocated by the new government may help; in all events the priority being given to domestic consumption as the principal driver of growth marks a major turning point in Japan's post-war economic policy.

3

JAPAN, AN ECONOMIC LEADER LOOKING FOR NORMALISATION

Despite the poor outlook for medium-term growth, Japan is still the dominant economic power in a rapidly integrating Asia. However, it has been the butt of cruel jibes in the past, derided as an economic giant but political dwarf whose regional and global influence in strategic terms bore no relation to its economic clout. The crisis of the 1990s made Japan aware of the limitations of defining its international position in purely economic terms; at the same time, far-reaching changes in the regional environment forced Tokyo to rethink its defence policy. Since then, Japan has aspired to a situation where it would be regarded not as an exception but as a normal country, taking diplomatic action and developing a defence capability commensurate with its economic strength.[1]

Asia's economic leader

Though the etymology of "Asia" continues to be a subject of debate, Herodotus used the term to refer to the East, meaning Asia Minor, then under Persian rule.[2] Even today, it corresponds more to a cultural concept of the Western mind than to a clearly defined geographical entity, because it does not reflect the extreme variety of countries and regions concerned. The Asia-Pacific region, which also includes Australasia and Oceania, represents about 25 per cent of world GDP, compared with 22 per cent for Asia per se and 20 per cent for East Asia.[3] East Asia has been responsible for over 40 per cent of world growth in the last ten years and its growing share of global output and trade has been accompanied by increasing integration of the region's economies. Japan plays a crucial role in the process, dominating an entire region whose development relies to a considerable extent on Japanese technology and investment. Japan's economic ties with China, the key vector of that regional integration, are particularly close because the region's two dominant economies are both complementary and dependent on each other.

East Asia on the path to economic integration

A patchwork of institutions

Economic integration is defined as the harmonisation of economic systems and the gradual removal of regulations that hinder the free movement of goods, services, capital and people. In Europe, the process has been driven primarily by political considerations and accomplished in several stages, from a customs union to a common market and a common currency. That is not the case with Asia. There is no formal institutional framework for Asian integration, which is functional rather than political. Unlike Europe, where the European Commission, an executive body, represents the common interest of the European Union (EU), Asia has no strong regional institutions; the consultation process is fragmented across a patchwork of organisations and forums. At the centre lies ASEAN and its ten member states,[4] linked by a free-trade agreement in the Asian Free-Trade Area (AFTA). Then comes ASEAN+3 (ASEAN Plus Three, APT), which includes China, South Korea and Japan as well as the 10

ASEAN countries. An informal grouping created in 1997 at the height of the Asian crisis, the APT is at the heart of the integration process and has spawned forty-nine consultative committees covering seventeen areas of cooperation. The annual East Asia Summit (EAS) brings together the APT countries with India, Australia and New Zealand in an ASEAN+6. Two consultation forums reach beyond Asia per se: ASEM (Asia-Europe Meeting), which provides a structure for dialogue between the APT and the EU, and APEC (Asia-Pacific Economic Cooperation), an economic forum for twenty-one Asian and Western countries on the Pacific Rim. The ARF (ASEAN Regional Forum) is a multilateral forum focusing on security issues in Asia whose twenty-seven members include the APT countries plus the EU, the United States, Canada, Russia, India, Pakistan and Australia. The Asian Development Bank (ADB), a member of the World Bank, also plays a role in financial integration and hosts the Asian Regional Integration Center (ARIC).

Several factors explain this web of organisations and the overlaps between the three main regional cooperation bodies, ASEAN, APT and EAS. Because nation-states did not emerge in Asia until relatively late, on account of colonisation, they are highly reluctant to cede any sovereignty at all to a supranational organisation. Furthermore, as the difficulties of extending ASEAN to its four most recent members (Cambodia, Laos, Myanmar and Vietnam) have shown, the integration process has to take account of great disparities, including different political regimes, diverging security options and, above all, dissimilarities of size and development level. But despite such differences, most members share similar development models, directly inspired by Japan.

The real catalyst of regional integration was the Asian crisis of 1997–98. The violence of that financial tsunami brought home the risk of contagion resulting from the increasing interdependence of the region's economies and hence their vulnerability to erratic movements of foreign capital. The integration process, hitherto entirely market-driven, took another direction, shifting towards a genuine, politically motivated regionalism and not merely the regionalisation of trade between private sector players. Although trade integration remains the cornerstone of regional construction, it is complemented by intergovernmental cooperation in the financial sphere. China and Japan have a decisive role to play in shaping the new order, an elliptical configuration of which they are the twin foci. It is only the beginning of a long process: the 2008–09 crisis underlined the limited options for any concerted action in the region, never mind coordinated stimulus plans. Those limits are due as much to the unspoken rivalry between China and Japan as to the lack of any real institutional framework for regional integration.

Trade integration

East Asia's international trade represents 26 per cent of total world trade, with Europe accounting for 39 per cent and NAFTA[5] for 16 per cent. Trade integration has made great strides since 1990. Intraregional trade has increased by a factor of eight, compared with five for the zone's total international trade and three for global trade, and now represents 57 per cent of trade in the region, compared with 73 per cent in the EU and 51 per cent in NAFTA. The structure of Asian trade has a number of distinctive and interlinked features. The first is the dependence of emerging Asian countries on exports, which have grown steadily over the last twenty years. With the rise of China and countries with very open economies like Hong Kong and Singapore, the share of exports in regional GDP has increased from 30 per cent in 1990 to 50 per cent now. Another distinctive feature is the double polarisation of regional trade. Trade is highly concentrated in certain sectors, such as electronics and telecommunications; furthermore, the proportion of intermediate goods is significantly higher than in NAFTA and the EU (60 per cent in Asia, 40 per cent in the EU). These semi-finished products (components, parts, etc.) are exported to another country in the zone for assembly as part of a vertical division of labour. China is the linchpin of the system, acting as a platform for exports: trade with China accounts for 60 per cent of the growth in regional trade over the last twenty years.

The third distinguishing feature of Asian trade is its triangular nature, which embodies the internal logic of the other two. This triangular process, seen above all in export industries such as electronic goods,[6] can be broken down into three stages: production of intermediate goods in one or more Asian countries, assembly in another and then export to the end market. The capital- and technology-intensive production of intermediate goods incorporates substantial value-added industry, whereas assembly is labour-intensive. Each country specialises in a segment of the value chain according to its comparative advantages: Japan and the NIACs[7] produce intermediate goods, China and the ASEAN countries import them for assembly and then export the finished products to end markets, especially Europe and the United States.[8] Half of Japan and China's foreign trade is with Asia because each one predominates at one end of the value chain: the former provides capital and technology, the latter the abundant cheap labour required for assembly.

Japanese multinationals have played a leading role since the 1980s in this regional division of labour (or "Asian integrated circuit") developing a dense network of production facilities throughout the region according to the imperatives of the day (economies of scale, presence on local markets, relocation due to labour costs or the appreciation of the yen, etc.). Thus, the expansion of regional trade in Asia is not so much a manifestation of political intent as the result of private sector strategy. However, the movement has been sustained by the liberalisation of trade achieved by governments through bilateral or regional free-trade agreements (FTAs).[9] ASEAN already has AFTA, while the Asia Pacific countries as a whole are either negotiating or have already concluded a total of 216 FTAs, 103 of them within the zone.[10] Although such agreements now cover about half of all regional trade, implementing them is inconsistent with the rationale of regional integration because their complexity (they have been compared to a "spaghetti bowl") hampers companies in the pursuit of a regional strategy. These bilateral agreements are much less effective than broad regional agreements because they reinforce the fragmentation of markets. It has been estimated that the formation of a vast free-trade area covering the entire Asia Pacific would generate an extra 1.3 points of growth on average for its members.[11] In 2006, Japan therefore put forward an ambitious plan for the creation of an Asia Pacific free-trade zone, CEPEA, as much to bolster its leading position in Asia as for reasons of economic efficiency. An economic partnership, CEPEA would embrace the sixteen ASEAN+6 countries and constitute the first step towards an East Asian Community. In October 2009, ASEAN+3 launched a feasibility study for the creation of a free-trade zone between its thirteen members and is conducting parallel discussions on closer economic cooperation with India, Australia and New Zealand.

The CEPEA plan is intended as a response to Chinese activism, which prevents Japan from claiming a position as the undisputed leader of the regional integration process. The free-trade agreement proposed in 2002 by the People's Republic of China (PRC) to the ten ASEAN countries came into force on 1 January 2010, with immediate effect for six of them. PRC-ASEAN trade more than tripled in five years, from USD 60 billion in 2003 to USD 178 billion in 2009, but the ASEAN deficit increased in the same proportion and now amounts to about USD 20 billion a year. The greatest effect of the almost complete lifting of customs barriers will be to boost Chinese exports of manufactured goods. This has aroused concern and reluctance in several countries, Indonesia foremost among them. Once again, Japan has been caught napping: its own free-trade agreement comes into piecemeal effect in the years up to 2012 according to the date of ratification by each member of ASEAN. Overall, the results of trade integration are mixed, with China emerging as the big winner from the other new division of labour in Asia and from globalisation. China's exports to the rest of the world increased by a factor of 6.6 between 1997 and 2007, those of ASEAN and Japan by only 2.5 and 1.7 respectively.[12] The sharp rise in foreign direct investment (FDI) in Asia has mostly benefited China, which has received three times more than ASEAN since 2000. The modest trade benefits for ASEAN, the crowding-out of FDI, and the jump in China's exports and FDI inflows beg the question of what advantages the less advanced countries can expect from the "Asian integrated circuit" in terms of technological progress. The risk is that fragmentation of the production cycle and the crushing weight of the region's three major economies[13]—including China, ASEAN's biggest customer—will keep them in a situation of dependence and leave them stuck at their current stage of development, on the lower rungs of the technological ladder.

Towards stability and financial autonomy

After the *anni mirabili* of the "Asian miracle" came the *anni horribili*: in 1997 and 1998, the "Asian crisis" devastated the region's economies and exposed the fragile foundations on which the miracle had been built. China and Japan were not directly affected but Japan had already been mired in its own crisis since the start of the decade. The Japanese crisis and the Asian crisis were very different both in their causes and in how they unfolded. The former lasted for over ten years, proceeding almost by stealth, at least until 1998; the latter was extremely violent but took only two years to surmount. Unlike the Japanese crisis, which was essentially of domestic origin, the Asian crisis was triggered by the dependence of Asia's emerging countries on foreign capital. That dependence precipitated the crisis: short-term foreign investors, attracted by the region's high-growth rates, fled at the first signs of economic downturn. The countries concerned recovered rapidly, but the structural reforms imposed by the IMF, in keeping with the "Washington consensus,"[14] imposed very heavy sacrifices on their people. The region's two heavyweights reacted responsibly and effectively: China by not devaluing despite the collapse of other Asian currencies, and Japan by providing financial support despite a domestic crisis that was exposing its banking sector to serious systemic risk.

The 1997–98 crisis opened a new chapter in the process of regional integration: that of monetary and financial cooperation. The devastating financial hurricane highlighted a number of shortcomings in the Asian model, including the risks of over-investment,[15] the dangers of over-rapid financial liberalisation for emerging countries and the fragility of the previous regional integration model. Under that model, trade links made the region's economies increasingly interdependent without any monetary coordination to protect them from the risk of contagion if one of their currencies collapsed.

Japan was the driving force behind the provision of financial support to crisis-stricken countries and the introduction of mechanisms for oversight and monetary coordination. To forestall any new crisis and ward off further IMF intervention, regarded as both too late and too harsh, in the autumn of 1997 Tokyo proposed the creation of an Asian Monetary Fund (AMF) with an initial endowment of USD 100 billion, of which it would contribute half. The United States and China immediately opposed the initiative, the former to preserve its financial influence in Asia through the IMF, at which it has a de facto right of veto, the latter to counter the dominant role that such a fund would have given Japan and the yen in a new monetary order in Asia. Following this rebuff, Tokyo offered the crisis countries financial assistance worth USD 30 billion in the "Miyazawa initiative" of October 1998. Despite their mixed results, Japan's unilateral initiatives paved the way for the monetary coordination that began within the APT framework in 2000. Under the "Chiang Mai Initiative" (CMI), central banks concluded currency swap agreements to provide each other with liquidity in the event of a foreign exchange crisis.

The agreements were concluded on a bilateral basis, country by country, but in May 2009, the APT decided to integrate them in a multilateral framework, CMIM, and pool the resources, hence enabling the creation of an emergency fund in the event of a monetary crisis. The USD 120 billion fund came into effect on 24 March 2010; with China and Japan each providing 32 per cent of the total, it resembles a more modest incarnation of the Asian Monetary Fund stillborn in 1997. Japan has made an additional USD 60 billion facility available for monetary swaps, raising its potential bill for supporting monetary stability in Asia to USD 100 billion. In a wider perspective, adding the USD 100 billion loan it offered to the IMF in November 2008, a rather surprising paradox emerges: the OECD country hardest hit by the crisis has been the most forthcoming in its help to Asian developing economies undermined by the global recession.

In addition to these defensive measures, the APT has started working on the wider integration of national financial markets, still very rudimentary in Asia (less than 20 per cent of foreign portfolio investment is made within the region, compared with 60 per cent in Europe). Vast reserves of savings leave the zone to be invested in foreign currencies because local financial markets are too narrow to absorb them.[16] The lack of large domestic bond markets means that companies have to make excessive use of costly bank lending; more widely, it means that savers in Asia are financing American consumers rather than the region's enormous infrastructure and social welfare needs. Consequently, through the Asian Bond Markets Initiative (ABMI), the APT is seeking to develop a regional bond market fed by issues denominated in local currencies that would increase not only the region's financial stability but also its autonomy.

In contrast, a common currency remains a very distant prospect, though the idea is regularly raised at APT meetings. There are huge economic disparities in the region and several of its currencies, including the yuan, are either partially or entirely non-convertible.[17] Even an intermediate stage as was the ECU[18] in Europe currently seems unachievable in Asia. Such a basket of currencies would have to be weighted according to economic indicators, on which it would be very difficult to achieve agreement. Pegging a unit of account to a regional benchmark currency would also raise the thorny problem of competition between the yuan and the yen, another major area of rivalry between China and Japan in the years to come. At present the yen has all the characteristics of an international currency, being at once a means of payment, a unit of account and a reserve currency; if its international use is limited, that is due only to Tokyo's wish to keep full control over monetary policy. Conversely, non-convertibility rules out the yuan, despite the free-trade agreement of 1 January 2010, which is likely to stimulate use of the currency within the region. Beijing recently offered certain countries the option of billing their bilateral trade with China in their national currencies and concluded swap agreements with Indonesia, Malaysia and South Korea. This advance heralds other steps towards full convertibility of the yuan and a liberalisation of exchange rate policy. Financial markets will also have to be developed, especially government bond markets, as they are currently too narrow to attract foreign investors.

Ultimately, the yuan could become an international reserve currency[19] in a quadripolar international monetary system (dollar, euro, yen, yuan) in which the dollar would play a reduced role but the United States would retain its "exorbitant privilege" of issuing the main global reserve currency for many years to come. In Asia, the yuan could impose itself as the regional currency, though Japan would of course oppose any such development and take steps to actively promote the yen. Leaving aside the question of the key currency, the prospect of monetary union brings us back to the crucial strategic issue for the two dominant powers: each considers that it should be the leader, China because of its global vision of international financial relations,[20] Japan because of its financial know-how and its position as Asia's pre-eminent economy.

Japan's economic predominance

Japan is Asia's pre-eminent economy in industrial, technological and financial terms. Supported by highly active economic diplomacy, Japan has imposed that pre-eminence through a dense network of companies and banks spanning the entire region. Japan is at the technological heart of emerging Asia's "integrated circuit" and has been largely responsible for financing its development. In a more diffuse way, and despite the scars of history, it sets an inescapable benchmark for Asian countries, most of which have borrowed its economic model. Even more generally, the influence of "Cool Japan"[21] is spreading throughout an Asia that looks for its cultural lead to Tokyo's Shibuya district, a magnet for the fashionable young.

Japanese firms at the heart of the "integrated circuit"

Japan has had a decisive influence on the structure of industry in Asia. Vertical integration between Japan, China and the rest of Asia owes much to Japanese production networks, which exported their domestic model to Asia. That model combines the fragmentation of manufacturing processes with highly centralised control of subsidiaries by the parent.[23] The value chain is fragmented between subsidiaries in different countries in the zone and procurement takes place within the group, including for partner subcontractors. Flows between subsidiaries are controlled by head office, which also provides central management functions. Research and development are often located in Japan, the role of subsidiaries being limited to adapting products to local markets. This model, both modular and centralised, is particularly well-suited to electronic goods and automobiles, sectors in which the technological content of components varies widely. Inspired by the internal organisation of vertically integrated industrial conglomerates (*keiretsu*) like Toyota, it uses the same management methods (flexibility, fluidity, quality control, continuous innovation, etc.).

It is a form of industrial organisation that has done much to shape the "Asian integrated circuit," distinguished by a high level of intra-firm exchanges. Upstream, factories in Japan export machine tools or high-value components,[24] while other parts of the value chain are divided between subsidiaries elsewhere in Asia according to the host country's comparative advantages. Downstream, a substantial proportion of output, especially from Chinese subsidiaries, is intended for the global market. Thus, the value-added goods exported by Japanese firms is augmented by the part that passes through the Asian integrated circuit, even if Japan's exports to the rest of the world remain stable in customs terms. Products manufactured by Japanese firms in countries like China and Thailand must be added to those produced in Japan in order to obtain a true measure of the value-added exported by Japan. With its strict hierarchies, this industrial model secures Japanese firms' supremacy in Asia because it is based on technological leadership and exceptional control over methods of production.

Japanese financial power and Asian development

Industry but also finance: these two factors of Asia's development are the instruments of Japan's dominant influence in the region. As the world's leading creditor nation and a major donor to multilateral institutions, Japan wields overwhelming financial power in Asia because it has the necessary capital, institutions and expertise. Its influence is exerted both through official assistance and through a close-knit network of private sector financial institutions throughout the region.

Japan had net public and private sector foreign assets worth almost USD 2.8 trillion at the end of 2009, compared with USD 1.8 trillion for China.[25] The size of its financial markets bears no relation to those in the rest of Asia: the Tokyo bond market is three times the size of all emerging Asia's bond markets put together and its stock market capitalisation is twice that of China and Hong Kong combined. Its great financial institutions are among the world's largest and can draw on both long experience and vast networks for their international operations. Until recently, three-quarters of their Asian subsidiaries were concentrated in Hong Kong (25 per cent), China (24 per cent), Singapore (17 per cent) and Thailand (16 per cent), but they have recently extended and diversified their networks, particularly in India, in order to take advantage of the opportunities offered by emerging countries in the region.

The expansion of private sector financial players has been compounded by the highly active economic diplomacy pursued by Tokyo in the region over the last thirty years, especially through official development assistance (ODA). Total ODA rose sharply during the 1980s, a geopolitical reflection of Japan's new standing as a global financial power. In 1989 Japan became the world's largest donor nation, ahead of the United States and France, and remained in that position for most of the 1990s. Budgetary restrictions have since reduced that contribution to its current level of 8 per cent of the world total.[26] Emerging Asian countries received over half Japan's ODA until the early 2000s, but that proportion has since fallen: Africa is now the leading recipient of Japanese ODA with 30 per cent of the total, Asia taking 28 per cent.

Japan is still the biggest donor to ASEAN countries and was long the leading donor to China, a fact rarely mentioned in the Chinese press. It is true, however, that the USD 35 billion paid to Beijing since 1979 is in lieu of war reparations and that assistance has been limited to technical cooperation for a number of years now. Emerging Asia's rise as a centre of industrial production and the development of its infrastructure owes much to Japanese assistance; that assistance is still crucial for the least advanced countries and makes a valuable contribution to the growing number of public-private partnerships (PPP) in the region. At a multilateral level, Japan has a decisive influence on the policy pursued by the Asian Development Bank (ADB), created in 1967 on the initiative of Japan, which nominates its president and has 17 per cent of the voting rights, the same as the United States. However, there is an area in which Japan has not sought to impose its supremacy. Despite paying lip-service to an internationalisation policy, Tokyo has not been able to bring itself to allow the yen to act as an international or even regional currency: it is used for only about 35 per cent of Japan's regional trade with Asia. Since the Asian crisis, in contrast, Japan has played a leading role in monetary coordination. Financial power is thus the second pillar of Japanese supremacy in Asia, resulting from a combination of several advantages: close links between private sector financial institutions and public economic cooperation bodies, influence in regional development organisations and deep involvement in projects to determine Asia's future financial architecture.

Soft power, Japanese-style

After industry and finance, can Japanese supremacy be said to rest on a third pillar, a "soft power" that enables Japan to leave its mark on countries in the region through its value system, its ideas, and its culture? The term "soft power" as defined by

Joseph Nye[27] would doubtless be inappropriate because Japan elicits ambivalent feelings in many Asian countries: mistrust of the former oppressor but also fascination with the success of an economic giant, despite its current misfortunes. In a broad sense, Japan exerts real cultural influence in Asia in two areas: its economic development model has greatly enhanced Japan's prestige in the region, while the "Cool Japan" style, especially pop culture, has won over Asian youth.

As mentioned previously, the Japanese model has largely inspired the development of Asian economies. Each country has replicated Japan's post-war export-oriented growth model according to its own particular characteristics. South Korean *chaebol* conglomerates have played a role similar to that of Japanese *keiretsu*. In China, foreign firms have driven the rise up the technology ladder, while in Hong Kong and Taiwan small family businesses have played a crucial part in industrialisation. The "flying geese paradigm," briefly described in connection with Japan in Chapter 2, helps to understand not only how industry took off in emerging Asian countries but also the current dynamic in the region, based on the vertical division of labour. Kaname Akamatsu's 1937 model analysed the product development cycle in an emerging country: import, local manufacture, export. Initially limited to a single product cycle, the paradigm has since been extended, first to comparative multisector analysis in a single country, then to multi-country analysis according to technological level. Activities can be seen to move from one country to another according to factors such as the country's level of industrial development and comparative advantages in terms of costs. Textiles manufacturing, for example, shifted from Japan to the NIACs, then to the ASEAN countries, and over time the process is repeated with other, more complex goods. The leading bird, in this case Japan, makes only the most sophisticated products. The model gives a reasonably robust account of the rise of industry in Asia, but China's move up-market has been rather different because the technological input of foreign firms has enabled it to skip certain steps.[28]

More generally, the Japanese economic model exerts its influence in a more diffuse way through seminars and conferences in Asia, attended by large numbers of Japanese senior civil servants and academics. All aspects of the Japanese experience are subject to detailed analysis at such gatherings, including the sources of its industrial and financial growth, of course, but also the disorders that led to the crisis of the 1990s.

Japanese influence in Asia has also spread through culture. METI's very earnest reports include assessments of the extent of the spread of Japanese cultural goods in Asia, which has almost doubled in ten years. Exports of films, manga, music and suchlike are worth almost USD 1 billion, with the four Dragons accounting for 70 per cent and China for 17 per cent. In regional terms, China, South Korea and Japan cooperate closely in matters concerning cultural goods. An annual forum involving private sector players and ministries aims to promote cooperation and regional partnerships in "content industries" (films, cartoons, TV programmes, music, video games, etc.). Thus, Japan spreads new forms of consumption in Asia, linking electronic devices and digital content. Japan is also a regional powerhouse for fashion, design and architecture, the Shanghai tower mentioned in the Introduction being just one illustration. In addition to generating income, the dissemination of Japanese cultural goods helps to reinforce the "Cool Japan" image among young people in Asia, far removed from the image they receive from their elders. Tokyo is well aware that soft power is another weapon in the battle for supremacy in Asia: Japan can boast not only democratic institutions that contrast with China's authoritarian regime but also an economic and cultural model that enhances its prestige and influence.

China and Japan: a relationship of dependence

China and Japan between them account for over three-quarters of East Asia's GDP, while China alone accounts for over half of emerging Asia's GDP. The economic relations between Asia's two giants are therefore the key to assessing the true extent of Japan's supremacy in the region. The structure of those relations is determined by mutual dependence in trade, investment and finance. Given the two countries' respective level of development, however, that interdependence is asymmetrical.

The growing integration of the two economies and China's parallel rise are the defining features of the last fifteen years or so. China's accession to the WTO in 2001 gave a massive boost to its foreign trade,[29] from which Japan was the main beneficiary, since China has become its main trade partner. Sino-Japanese trade has doubled in value since 2000: 20 per cent of Japan's trade is now with China, compared with 13 per cent in 2000 and 7 per cent in 1995. On the Chinese side, trade with Japan, its leading supplier, represents 10 per cent of the total. Unlike the United States and Europe, Japan's trade with China/ Hong Kong is balanced. Their trade integration stems from the broader process of regional integration, which here achieves its full effect since the development gap between the two economies makes them complementary in terms of both markets and products. Japan exports goods with a high technological content, such as machine tools and electronic components, and imports products with less value-added, such as textiles, agricultural products and consumer electronics.[30] The complementarity in the trade between Japan and China is due, as we have seen, to the effect of their comparative advantages in an almost ideal configuration, with advanced technology on one side and low-cost labour on the other.

For the same reason, there is still little competition between their products on markets in the developed world, as the absence of disputes before the WTO indicates. On closer examination, however, China's trade positions appear to be progressing very rapidly at Japan's expense: Chinese exports of manufactured goods rose from 6 to 14 per cent of the world market between 1995 and 2005, while Japan's market share fell by four points, from 14 to 10 per cent over the same period.[31] However, these customs statistics give only a partial account of the real situation because Chinese export figures include products manufactured by Japanese companies in China. A similar reasoning applies to an assessment of the extent of each country's dependence in trade matters. At first sight it looks as though Japan is more dependent, since 18 per cent of its exports go to China whereas Japan absorbs only 8 per cent of Chinese exports, considerably less than the United States and Europe (18 per cent each). But while the Chinese market is essential for Japan's growth, China is probably more reliant on Japan than vice versa: its industrial and commercial expansion relies to a considerable extent on the technology it imports from Japan in the form of intermediate goods (components, etc.) or capital goods (machinery, etc.).

The trade integration of the two economies reflects the vertically integrated production networks described earlier. That division of labour and the intra-firm exchanges it engenders leave China technologically dependent on Japanese companies, the Chinese subsidies of which have tripled in number in ten years. Most of Japan's top 1,000 industrial firms have factories in China. They have remained cautious in their relocation strategies, however, and diversified their risks in Asia to avoid any excessive dependence. China accounts for only 8 per cent of Japan's stock of FDI worldwide; the equivalent figure for the ASEAN countries is 11 per cent, for Europe 27 per cent and for the United States 32 per cent. Japan's share of foreign investment in China, excluding Hong Kong, does not exceed 11 per cent. That caution is matched by a highly selective approach to relocated activities, which generally exclude research and development. Extremely mindful of intellectual property issues, Japan is the leading foreign investor in terms of patents filed in China, with 44 per cent of the total.[32]

The extensive integration of these two dominant economies, at once complementary and interdependent, thus marks a major turning point in the regional configuration. Yet China and Japan have not signed or even contemplated a free-trade agreement,[33] even though they are keen to conclude FTAs with many other countries in the region. The agricultural component of any such agreement is one obstacle, given the poor productivity of Japanese farmers. Above all, however, the two partners can foresee fierce competition in each other's domestic markets. Competition between Chinese and Japanese exporters, currently weak in developed countries but already keen in emerging countries,[34] will intensify as China makes up for its technology lag. The Japanese market will not be immune from Chinese competition, so Tokyo has no interest in opening it up too soon. At present, competition is taking place above all in the strategic area of access to natural resources, as can be seen with oil in Siberia and the exploitation of hydrocarbon deposits in the East China Sea. In the future, that competition will play out in the arena of technology: that, at least, is China's ambition, and the greatest threat to Japan's supremacy.

Japan's aspiration to "normalisation"

Japan occupies a peculiar position both geographically and strategically. Although part of Asia, it very soon chose the West as an essential step on the path to modernity. It is also the only nation in the world to have renounced a sovereign right and an essential attribute of power, that of ensuring its own security. Japan's ambivalence towards its own identity and the transfer to its American protector of its right to "legitimate violence" are the shaping factors of a foreign policy that is often difficult to interpret because it oscillates between contradictory demands. Japanese policy towards Asia is subject to tension between regionalism and multilateralism; its international positioning as a civilian power is pulled between structural dependence on the United States for its defence and a demand for autonomy in the exercise of active pacifism for the promotion of global public goods. To cope with these pressures, Tokyo has built its foreign policy on two main foundations: a renewed focus on Asia and an active pacifism that seeks to reconcile a military alliance with the United States with the promotion of multilateralism within the UN.

A renewed focus on Asia

The 1947 Constitution, mostly drafted by the occupying Americans, turned Japan into a liberal democracy, but renouncing war and all armed force was the price the country had to pay for keeping its emperor and its imperial institutions. The only Western-style democracy in Asia, Japan is tethered to the United States through its constitution and, above all, through the 1951 Japan-US Security Treaty, renewed and clarified in 1960. Having renounced the right to defend itself, Japan would henceforth depend on the United States to preserve its security. The "Yoshida doctrine"[35] defined Japan's relations with other countries: turned towards a West they were seeking to catch up with, Japan's leaders would devote themselves to economic expansion, the only weapon available to the country in its relations of force with the rest of the world.

The renewed focus on Asia began in the late 1970s with the "Fukuda doctrine," which defined three guidelines for Japan's Asian policy: first, renunciation of all military ambition; second, mutual relations founded on trust; and third, cooperation on an equal footing rooted in links of friendship rather than economic imperatives. The shift in focus became fully operative in the early 1990s under the combined effect of several factors, including the collapse of the Soviet Union, the rise of China and an economic crisis at home. The reordering of strategic priorities was marked by a highly symbolic event. A contingent of troops was dispatched to Cambodia in 1992 as part of the UN peacekeeping operation there, sending the message to Asia that Japan intended to be a responsible and useful regional power, not only anxious to protect its economic interests but also willing to work for stability and peace. The move also marked a turning point in Tokyo's defence policy: a taboo was lifted and, for the first time since the Second World War, troops—albeit unarmed—were sent overseas under the terms of the Peacekeeping Operations Act passed in 1992.[36] This strategic return to Asia was accompanied by growing involvement in regional security issues, especially after 1998, when the threat from North Korea became more pressing. Economic diplomacy, regional construction and security issues would henceforth be the three main priorities of Japan's foreign policy in Asia.

A partial conversion to regionalism

Economic diplomacy (*keizai gaikō*) is Japan's forte and its neighbours dispute neither its legitimacy nor its effectiveness, whatever their misgivings in other areas. Official development assistance plays a key role. Economic by nature, ODA also has a political dimension because decisions to grant aid are taken on the basis of criteria such as the recipient's track record on defence spending and armaments, the level of democracy and respect for human rights, progress towards a market economy and respect for the environment. China's proactive promotion of free-trade agreements may have caught Japan off guard, but it is trying hard to make up lost ground. In contrast, Japan plays a pivotal role in regional monetary and financial integration. Drawing on its financial power and, even more so, its international experience of monetary systems, Japan has so far acted as the mainspring for financial coordination in the ASEAN+3 framework. Despite Chinese and American rejection of its proposal for an Asian Monetary Fund in 1998, the support it gave to crisis-stricken countries at the time and its repeated initiatives in favour of better monetary coordination have won Japan esteem and respect in the region. And yet its economic diplomacy in Asia remains ambivalent. Japan fears finding itself imprisoned in an "Asian fortress" and would like to see an open form of regionalism that would enable it to keep its privileged relations with the United States. That is why Tokyo presents itself as an ardent champion of Asia Pacific Economic Cooperation (APEC). Japan sees APEC, a forum for partners that represent two-thirds of its trade, as an ideal consultation body, which enables it to reconcile the fact of being an Asian country with membership of the developed nations club.[37]

An ambitious vision of regional construction

Japan was made brutally aware of its fragile position in the international and regional pecking order when Presidents Clinton and Jiang Zemin declared in October 1997 that they wished to build a strategic partnership between China and the United States. Since then, the horizons of Japanese diplomacy have been bounded by rivalry with an omnipresent China. That is especially the case with regional construction, the central tenet of the DPJ's Asian policy. The two countries have a different vision of a future Asian Community, and especially of where its geographical boundaries might lie. In 2005, Tokyo managed to impose the East Asia Summit (EAS) as the main regional coordination body (inappropriately named, it spans ASEAN+6 and also includes India, Australia and New Zealand). China had lobbied for ASEAN+3, where its influence is greater. In the Japanese view, economic integration between the sixteen EAS countries would be the first stage in a more ambitious project that would then be extended to the political and strategic realm. For Tokyo, ASEAN must play a central role: it must be the driving force behind a process that will doubtless take several decades, given the disparities between the countries concerned, their conflicting interests and ASEAN's structural weaknesses in political and operational terms.

Tokyo's support for an extended Asian Community plainly reflects its desire to contain Beijing's growing influence in the region. Its strategy is therefore to draw on the "arc of democracy" that unites Japan, India, Australia, New Zealand and the United States, de facto excluding China (at least under its current regime).[38] The recent rapprochement between Japan and India can be explained by their complementary ambitions in an Asia moving towards integration. India, with its economic potential, democratic tradition and military resources, sees itself as a major power in the region; like Japan, it fears the formation of an Asia under Chinese domination. The four-day visit to Tokyo by India's prime minister, Manmohan Singh, in December 2006 allowed the two countries to define the main thrusts of a global, economic and strategic partnership. At international level, both India and Japan wish to become permanent members of the UN Security Council in recognition of their status as major powers. At regional level, India, as one of Asia's emerging great powers, is a rival in the making for China, while Japan wishes to integrate it into regional organisations to act as a counterweight to Beijing.

By teaming up with India, the third great Asian power, Japan could thus steer the options for Asian integration in two directions: the creation of a vast Asia-Pacific free-trade area, as Tokyo proposed in 2006, and coordination in monetary and financial matters, where Japan would obviously play a major role. India and Japan share the same concerns about security in Asia and will work together closely in this area.[39] Their strategic partnership was given formal expression on 22 October 2008 in a cooperation pact that covers matters such as the security of sea lanes, the fight against terrorism, peacekeeping operations, disaster management, disarmament and non-proliferation. It is the only agreement of this type to have been concluded by Japan to date, except for those already in force with the United States and Australia. India is thus a key partner for Japan in its quest to influence the regional architecture, since Tokyo considers that the two countries "share the same values" of democracy and human rights, which must form the basis of a "new order" in Asia founded on the "arc of democracy."[40]

Growing threats and regional security

With ASEAN, Japan was the driving force behind the creation in 1994 of the ASEAN Regional Forum (ARF), whose members include the Asia-Pacific countries, the United States, the European Union and Russia. However, it remains convinced that the alliance with the United States[41] offers the best guarantee against regional threats to its security, from North Korea in the immediate future and perhaps from China at some later stage.[42]

North Korea (the Democratic People's Republic of Korea) is a major challenge for Japan because it is geographically close and poses a variety of threats. The Pyongyang regime has a proven ballistic missile capability and its nuclear potential was confirmed after a second underground test in May 2009. Its arsenal of chemical and biological weapons does nothing to relieve a feeling of extreme vulnerability in Tokyo, which suffered a traumatic poison gas attack by the Aum sect in 1995. The problem is compounded by the highly sensitive issue of the Japanese citizens kidnapped by Pyongyang in the 1970s and 80s to help train North Korean agents for future missions in Japan. With the United States, the two Koreas, Russia and China, Japan is a participant in the Six-Party Talks, which aim to negotiate a halt to

North Korea's nuclear programme in return for American support for its nuclear power industry and massive aid, especially from Japan. Pyongyang's real intentions can only be a matter of speculation. Some analysts argue that the nuclear programme is purely defensive and intended to be used as a means of blackmailing Washington in order to obtain a peace treaty, a security commitment and economic aid.

Japan had hoped that Beijing would prove a more effective mediator with a regime accustomed to using blackmail and provocation. Tokyo's disappointment on that front has been compounded by a form of resentment against Washington: perceived as being too soft on China on the issue of North Korea, the US administration is also regarded as downplaying the problem of the kidnapped Japanese citizens, which has a very strong symbolic resonance in Japan. More generally, the threat from North Korea causes Japan to reflect upon the meaning of its pacifism in such a context, and to a considerable extent explains its shift towards a more active stance on defence. Tokyo feels all the more isolated on the North Korean issue in that it also regards South Korea as being too conciliatory towards its northern neighbour since the launch in 1998 of a normalisation policy (the "Sunshine Policy"). Relations between Tokyo and Seoul are strained, not least by unhealed historical wounds and territorial disputes, especially as there is little real economic complementarity between the two countries to soften the hard edges, contrary to the situation between Tokyo and Beijing. Japan's relationship with the two Koreas thus highlights the limitations and dilemmas of Japanese foreign policy in its renewed focus on Asia: the weight of the past hampers Tokyo's diplomatic and strategic ambitions in the region, and its isolation vis-à-vis the North Korean threat is forcing Japan to cast off its passive pacifism.

The second threat, that of China, is doubtless less immediate, but two issues in particular cause concern in Tokyo: the tripling of China's defence budget since 2000 and the 2005 Anti-Secession Law, authorising military intervention if Taiwan were to declare independence. If the United States were to intervene following a PRC invasion of Taiwan, Japan could find itself indirectly involved in armed conflict. The new defence cooperation guidelines concluded with the United States in 1997 extend the scope of action of Japan's Self-Defence Forces, which could now cooperate with the US Army outside Japan in the event of regional conflict. They would have a strictly non-combat role, but the wording is sufficiently vague to leave plenty of scope for interpretation.[43] Another of Tokyo's concerns is China's defence spending since 2000, and especially its lack of transparency.[44] Tokyo has trouble understanding the reasoning of the Beijing regime, which emphasises the peaceful nature of China's "rise" while tripling its defence budget in eight years. Apart from the possibility of being dragged into a conflict over Taiwan, Japan fears that the sudden increase in its neighbour's military capability might one day threaten its vital interests, especially the security of its shipping lanes. The threats against its security are forcing it to emerge from passive pacifism under American protection and to come up with a new strategic stance in Asia. The process has been under way for a number of years and could accelerate under a DPJ government. It remains to be seen how the DPJ will strike a balance between an avowed desire for greater involvement in Asia and the alliance with the United States. The DPJ government appears to have little room for manoeuvre in relation to the strategic options and foreign policy already in place since the mid-1990s, namely a more active defence policy in Asia and the promotion of public goods at a global level.

Active pacifism within the UN framework

Japan's dilemma is how to reconcile the pacifism imposed by its Constitution with the desire to be recognised as a global power in the same way China is, albeit on a different level. It is seeking to overcome this contradiction in a novel way: benefiting from American military protection, Japan wishes to assert itself as a great civilian power, serving the cause of peace and global public good within the framework of the United Nations.

American protection but greater defensive capacities

From Raymond Aron's realistic standpoint, "power is, in the broadest sense, the capacity to act, to produce, to destroy."[45] By that yardstick, Japan has clearly deprived itself of an essential attribute of power, since in its 1947 Constitution it renounced the capacity to destroy and hence to ensure its own security.

Article 9 of the Constitution precisely summarises the radical nature of Japan's demilitarisation and the pacifism that justifies it. In the first paragraph, the Japanese people "forever renounce war [...] and the threat or use of force as a means of settling international disputes"; the second paragraph contains an undertaking not to maintain armed forces or "other war potential." In return for that loss of sovereignty, the 1951 Security Treaty with the United States gives Japan the assurance of American military protection.[46] The strategic configuration of this "passive" pacifism lasted for thirty years. Relieved of the financial burden of military spending, Japan was able to put its efforts into expanding its economy. Stripped of strategic power, it became an economic giant with the foreign policy of a "merchant" nation, seeking what Robert Scalapino[47] has called "maximum profit and minimum risk." Trade relations with the United States became increasingly tense in the 1980s as the Americans imposed far-reaching reforms of trade and monetary policy on their Japanese ally. On defence, the American position evolved rapidly after the 1951 Treaty: from 1954, Japan was ordered to "share the burden" of its defence and decided to transform its police force into a self-defence force (SDF). An embryo army in all but name, it has a purely defensive role, limited to Japanese soil. Japan's defence doctrine at the time was based on a set of principles that defined the SDF's nature and functions: no offensive capability, no exports of arms or military-use technologies, no manufacture, use or presence of nuclear weapons on Japanese soil,[48] renunciation of collective legitimate defence.

A break with this defence policy came in the early 1990s. Having responded to US demands to share the burden of its defence, Japan sought to assert itself on the international stage. Hitherto a passive ally, Tokyo wanted to be not only a partner of the United States but also a strategic player in its own right. Given the restrictions written into Japan's constitution, the only way open was that of multilateralism in the framework of the United Nations. From 1992, Japan started taking part in UN peacekeeping operations and sent SDF contingents abroad on humanitarian support missions.[49] However, the alliance with the United States remains the anchor of Japanese foreign policy, as can be seen from its support for the wars in Iraq and Afghanistan,[50] and the joint development with the United States of an anti-missile shield due to come into operation in 2011.

In view of these developments, the text of the 1947 Constitution needs to be brought into line with the realities of 2010, a highly sensitive subject both within Japan and elsewhere. The DPJ, now in power, is itself divided on the issue but a revision will be essential to end the casuistical paradox whereby a constitutional ban on all "war potential" is reconciled with the existence of a powerful army, albeit one called a "self-defence force." The transformation in 2006 of the Defence Agency into a fully-fledged ministry marked a symbolic first step. The 250,000 members of the SDF seem to weigh little in the balance against China's army of 2.3 million, but Japan's defence budget is the world's fifth-largest. Limited by an unwritten rule to less than 1 per cent of GDP, it amounted to USD 58 billion in 2010 compared with China's USD 78 billion. Professional and well trained, the SDF has sophisticated equipment and is well ahead of China's armed forces on that score. Recent Defence Ministry projects, including spy satellites, the anti-missile shield and helicopter-carrying destroyers, point to its determination to use all the country's technological resources to back up its detection and intervention capabilities.

A civil nuclear power, Japan intends to remain a conventional military power with a purely defensive capability. It therefore lacks the capacity for deterrence that gives the great military powers, especially China, an essential edge. The nuclear option is ruled out in the current geopolitical environment but the question is no longer taboo,[51] and there is no guarantee that this final step towards "normalisation" will not be taken one day. Japan depends for its protection on the US nuclear umbrella, an in-built dependence that obviously imposes limits on its diplomatic action. The change of government is not likely to bring about any major change in a defence policy founded on the alliance with the United States. It is true that a new generation of politicians less sensitive to the "special relationship" with the United States is emerging; foreign policy is less likely to depend on Washington than in the past. A former Japanese diplomat has neatly summarised the limits that constitute a stumbling-block for any strengthening of the alliance: "The two partners still lie in the same bed, but they no longer dream the same dreams." Yukio Hatoyama indicated during his campaign that he wanted Japan to grow away from the United States and turn more towards Asia. From his standpoint, it was the only way for the country to extricate itself from the dilemma it faces: "How should Japan maintain its political and economic independence and protect its national interest when caught between the United States ... the world's dominant power, and China which is seeking ways to become one?"[52] In power, Hatoyama nevertheless hastened to reassure Washington, declaring that "the US-Japan alliance is the foundation of Japanese diplomacy." President

Obama, during his visit in November 2009, was at pains to placate Tokyo, explaining that closer relations between China and the United States in a "pragmatic cooperation" did not imply any weakening in the system of American alliances in Asia. In fact, Washington seems to want to differentiate the roles it attributes to Beijing and Tokyo, with China being a discussion partner on major international issues and Japan a counterweight to Chinese ambitions. Significant tensions have emerged between Tokyo and Washington over certain aspects of the alliance, such as the presence of American bases on Japanese soil,[53] logistical support in the Indian Ocean,[54] and Yukio Hatoyama's failed attempt to move the US military base at Futenma, which hastened his downfall. Even if the 1960 US-Japan Security Treaty which remains the cornerstone of Japan's defence policy,[55] Japan wishes to turn its constitutionally self-imposed pacifism into the "active" pacifism of a great civilian power.

A great civilian power, sincere but ambiguous

In a speech at the United Nations on 24 September 2009, the then Japanese prime minister, Yukio Hatoyama, set out his conception of the international role he intended to promote for his country. According to him, Japan has a unique and essential role to play in the world: a developed Asian country and a pacifist power, the "new Japan" should act in "a spirit of fraternity" (yuai) to become "a bridge for the world, between the Orient and the Occident, between developed and developing countries, ... between states possessing nuclear weapons and those without them." It would take action in five areas: economic revival and a greater international role in promoting more balanced global growth; leadership on climate change issues; initiatives for nuclear disarmament and non-proliferation; action to build peace and eradicate poverty; and the construction of an Asian community. The vocabulary and certain turns of phrase were new, but for the most part Hatoyama was following the same line as some of his predecessors. Having renounced military force, Japan aims to take its rightful place as a great civilian power and believes it has the necessary qualities for that, including economic muscle, the choice of multilateral diplomacy in crisis prevention and management, and the primacy of supranational institutions in laying down law and setting standards.[56]

Japan's economic and financial might enabled the country to become a member of the G7 on its inception and has been reflected in substantial contributions to international organisations. An "active" pacifist, it has also sought to be a "useful" one. At the other end of the spectrum from neo-realism and closer to constructivism, Japan believes in international cooperation rather than confrontation; in disarmament rather than deterrence. Without any universalist pretensions, it campaigns for the respect of different cultures; at a time when religions are being perverted by fundamentalism, its syncretism and tolerance may appear as premises of an art of living together that transcends ethnic and religious divides. Drawing on its economic power and the moral legitimacy of its pacifism, Japan endeavours to promote global public goods, human security, peacebuilding and respect for the environment. On the latter point in particular, its legitimacy is unrivalled because it has succeeded in combining economic growth with energy efficiency and respect for the environment through its exceptional mastery of innovative technologies. On 22 September 2009, at the UN climate change summit, Yukio Hatoyama announced the target of a 25 per cent reduction in greenhouse gas emissions by 2020 in relation to 1990, easily the most ambitious of all the developed nations. He was also the first to propose a specific mechanism for financing the reduction of emissions by emerging countries (the "Hatoyama initiative"), a major step forward before the calamitous Copenhagen summit in December 2009.

But although Japan has indeed become a major civilian power, its position is not entirely unambiguous. Its generous development aid and substantial contributions to international institutions are also instruments of power that help to promote its own strategic or trade interests. Japan may have been able to distance itself from US positions on the International Criminal Court or the Kyoto Protocol, for example, but the independence of its policy on Iran and the Middle East is dictated more by national interest than by the values it promotes in other areas: it depends on Saudi Arabia for 28 per cent of its oil supplies, on the United Arab Emirates for 25 per cent and on Iran for 12 per cent.[57] There is also another side to its lack of universalist pretensions: an acute sense of the unique nature of Japanese identity is a prism that can alter its vision of the world and obscure the importance of certain issues. More generally, the ambivalence of its strategic positioning can be explained by an incomplete process of "normalisation." Japan is seeking to enhance its international standing and escape from the straitjacket of passive pacifism. It wishes to restore national pride by turning the page on a past for which China constantly reproaches it. It is casting around for a way to put an end to the "Japanese exception" and become a "normal" country with a defence capability to match its economic muscle and the threats to its security. However, that aspiration soon comes up against the constitutional restriction that deprives it of strategic power; its pacifism, even active, limits Japan's arsenal to purely defensive conventional weapons and influence diplomacy.

In July 2005, together with the other members of the G4 (Brazil, India and Germany), Japan asked to be admitted as a permanent member of the UN Security Council as part of a reform that was ultimately postponed. China campaigned against Japan's request on the grounds of what it called the resurgence of Japanese "militarism." Yet Japan's economic weight and its action in seeking solutions to major international problems may be seen as fully qualifying it for such a role. Pressure is increasing, especially from France, for a gradual reform of the Security

Council, whose permanent members would ultimately include the current five plus Germany, Brazil, India, Japan and a major African nation. Judging by the joint communiqué issued by the Chinese and Japanese prime ministers, Wen Jiabao and Shinzo Abe, on 11 April 2007, it is possible that China would no longer oppose such a solution: "The two sides agreed to enhance dialogue and consultation on UN reform and strive to expand common ground. China is ready to see Japan playing a bigger and constructive role in international affairs."

4

CHINA, A GLOBAL POWER IN THE MAKING

Whatever the rhetoric of "peaceful rise" (*heping jueqi*),[1] the Chinese Communist Party knows that its legitimacy, and hence its survival, depends on two key factors. They are the pursuit of strong economic growth and the assertion of Chinese power in both Asia and the world as a whole, the first being the prerequisite for the second. As a first step, China aims to impose itself as Asia's undisputed leader, in both economic and strategic terms. It therefore needs not only to supersede Japan as the dominant power but also to undermine American influence in the region and thwart the ambitions of a Japan whose desire for "normalisation" is equivalent in Chinese eyes to the resurgence of militarism. A race with Japan on the economic front and diplomatic activism are thus the twin strands of China's strategy in Asia.

For China, however, the ambition of Asian supremacy is just one aspect of a broader pursuit of global power, because Beijing is driven by a global not regional vision of the world. That thinking was already present in Mao's dream at the time of the Great Leap Forward in 1958: catching up with the United States in fifteen years. The dream will probably not be realised until around 2030 in terms of GDP by volume, but China's successive "helmsmen" have steadfastly set their sights on America. A superpower in the making, China aims ultimately to challenge American hegemony and to influence the world order in a dialogue of equals, if not a confrontation, with the United States. Despite Deng Xiaoping's reassuring speech to the United Nations General Assembly in 1974—"China is not a superpower, nor will she ever seek to be one"—the final destination to which the Chinese compass points is indeed the United States.

The race for economic supremacy in Asia

The G20 summit in November 2008 showed that the rich country club had opened its membership to the major powers of the future. The symbolic impact of the summit in April 2009 was even greater, underlining just how far China had broken into the ruling circle of a new world in the making. China's president was everywhere, overshadowing a mute and unobtrusive Japan, while the participation of the leading emerging nations prefigured forthcoming upsets in the hierarchy of the great powers. Yet Japan's economic supremacy in Asia is based not primarily on the size of its economy but on its lead in technology. Beijing may be engaged in a race to overtake Japan in this respect, but the outcome is far from certain.

Upsets in the hierarchy of the great powers

According to a Goldman Sachs study of the BRIC emerging powers updated in 2007, China is likely to become the world's largest economy by around 2030,[2] or perhaps even 2027.[3] If so, in less than twenty years China would find itself back in the position it occupied in the early nineteenth century. It would stand at the top of a new world ranking, followed by the United States, India and Japan, whose economy by then would be a quarter the size of its much larger neighbour. Though China would have regained its power, standards of living would still be much lower than in the United States, Europe or Japan: income per capita would be only 28 per cent of the American figure and 35 per cent of the Japanese figure, compared with 10 per cent at present. The GDP gap would widen considerably by 2050, since China's GDP would theoretically be twice that of the United States and ten times that of Japan, with income per capita equivalent to that of the United States today.

Despite the unreliability of such very long-term forecasts, noted in the Introduction, some underlying trends are clear and may be summarised in three points. First, the rise of the emerging powers will profoundly change the structure of global production: output from the BRICs could have outstripped that of the G7 within twenty years, and by 2050 the American and Japanese economies will doubtless be the only ones left from the current top six. Second, unless China experiences major political and social upheaval, it could become the world's largest economy by around 2030; GDP per capita would have increased fivefold to USD 17,500, equivalent to a third that of Japan by that time or half that of Japan now. Third, despite a very high standard of living, Japan would be rapidly relegated to the status of a medium-sized power as measured by the yardstick of Chinese GDP, which overtook Japan's in 2010.

The fact that China has caught up with Japan marks a major turning point for both countries. Whether or not China becomes the world's largest economy within twenty years remains a distant prospect subject to numerous imponderables, but the fact that it has overtaken Japan as the world's second-largest economy has a powerful and immediate symbolic impact, not least as a form of revenge. Yet the reversal of positions is in the order of things, given that China's workforce is twelve times larger than Japan's: an existing set of forces is simply playing out in a purely mechanical way. It does not mean that China has caught up with Japan in qualitative terms, however, because the criterion of GDP per capita underlines the enormous productivity gap that separates the two economies, and will continue to do so for many years to come. From that standpoint, China is still a developing country. That is partly due to the size of the agricultural sector,[4] but even more to the difference in terms of technological progress. In preserving its supremacy, Japan's trump card is its tremendous technological lead, which derives from a system of continuous innovation. The important thing now for China, as much as and perhaps even more than continuing strong growth, is the technological quality of that growth.

The criterion of technological excellence

The arena in which Japan can take on China is not that of size, whether of population or the economy, for that battle has already been lost, but of global supremacy in terms of innovation and creativity. Though it will soon be only a medium-sized economic power, Japan has no intention of relinquishing its position as the world's leader in technology to China, which has already set itself highly ambitious objectives in that area for 2020.

Japan's lead in technology

Many different parameters are involved in the measurement of technological prowess, but whatever the methodology used, Japan systematically comes out on top. The classification produced by the Economist Intelligence Unit (EIU),[5] for example, takes into account not only key innovation factors such as funding and the number of researchers but also outcomes in terms of patents, articles published and cited, etc. Japan's global supremacy in research and development (R&D) is reflected in the record number of patents filed by Japanese firms. On that criterion, eight Japanese companies number in the world's top ten.[6] They account for 22 per cent of patents filed in the United States, and the 2008 ranking of the top ten companies by number of patents includes five Japanese and only three American firms. For "triadic" patents (patents filed simultaneously in Japan, the United States and Europe), Japan is on a par with the United States and the European Union, registering an annual average of 14,000 patents, 29 per cent of the world total.[7] In terms of technological density (the number of patents in relation to the size of the economy and the population), Japan is easily the world leader ahead of Switzerland, with 120 triadic patents per million inhabitants per year as against fifty-five for the United States and thirty-three for Europe. It has greatly extended its lead over the last fifteen years, since the 1995 figure was just seventy-five. Japan's technological balance of payments (purchases and sales of licences), in deficit until 1990, now shows a substantial surplus. Annual licence sales exceeded USD 20 billion in 2008, compared with purchases of USD 6 billion.[8] Seventy per cent of sales are to the United States and are concentrated in high-technology sectors, especially electronics, mechanical engineering, fine chemicals, new nanostructured materials,[9] energy and the environment. In the energy/environment sector, for example, photovoltaic patent applications accounted for 68 per cent of the world total as against 15 per cent for Europe and 11 per cent for the United States. Japan also registered 72 per cent of electric and hybrid vehicle patents, compared with Europe's 14 per cent.[10] In contrast, there are sectors like pharmaceuticals in which Japan does very little research.[11]

The quest for technological supremacy began in the 1980s. Since then, long-term fundamental research programmes have been launched and competitiveness clusters established nationwide. Japan excels not only in microelectronics and nanotechnologies[12] but also in mixed technologies. Combining different elements such as electronics with mechanical engineering in mechatronics or with optics in optronics, these technologies create new markets. As a form of "techno-globalism," they flourish in multidisciplinary research centres like the Tsukuba Research

117

Consortium. Humanoid robotics, a field in which Japanese researchers have made impressive progress, is a good example. In January 2008, a humanoid robot in a Kyoto laboratory was able to reproduce the movements of a monkey walking on a treadmill in Durham in the United States. The computer in Durham sent the signals directing the motion from the monkey's brain to the robot's computer in Kyoto, which turned them into instructions for movements. The project, carried out in cooperation with Duke University in the United States, could lead to highly innovative applications such as artificial legs controlled by the wearer's brain or rescue robots that can work by remote control or in hostile environments.[13]

Japanese firms do not only develop new products: they are also expert at optimising industrial processes. *Monozukuri* (literally the "art of making things," it is described as a quintessence of science, technology and skill) lies at the heart of an innovation system that is gaining in complexity as the value chain becomes more fragmentary and production processes more modular. In this situation, the capacity to innovate is no longer limited to technical knowledge but embraces interactive management of the various stages of production. This extended concept of the innovation process, which is the source of value creation, results in "black box" technologies which are difficult for rivals to imitate, not only because they are protected by intellectual property rights but also, and above all, because they incorporate unique production methods and control technologies.[14] Big names like Sony, Matsushita and Canon are only the visible tip of a technological iceberg made up of thousands of medium-sized companies applying a niche strategy of specialising in specific segments or components. Some of them can hold a dominant share of the world market—in some cases as much as 70–80 per cent—for products whose technological content is so great that there is no real competition.

Japan accounts for about 20 per cent of the world's R&D expenditure despite having only 2 per cent of its population. The research budget, 77 per cent of which is company-funded, represents 3.4 per cent of GDP compared with an OECD average of 2.3 per cent, and Japan has 11.1 researchers per 1,000 workers against 9.6 in the United States and 8.2 in France. Only 12 per cent of R&D spending is devoted to fundamental research: Japan's real success lies in applied research, which takes up the lion's share of resources. Japanese research draws its strength from the money poured into it by private firms: 2.7 per cent of GDP as against 1.8 per cent in the United States and 1.1 per cent in the European Union. However, the effectiveness of research spending has tended to decrease over the years due to a more competitive international research environment and the shortcomings of the Japanese system, namely the concentration of research in very large firms, a relative shortage of venture capital and little international cooperation. Alarm signals send out regular reminders of the strength of competition, including from within Asia. Yet Japan's technological supremacy is not under real threat from the advances made in Taiwan or South Korea. To give an example, the index that measures the technological content of exports remained more or less flat for South Korea between 2000 and 2009 but rose by 35 per cent for Japan.[15] If a threat were to arise one day it would be from the ambitions Beijing now harbours in that sphere, but China has so much ground to catch up that Japan's supremacy seems unlikely to be challenged for at least the next fifteen years or so.

China's quest for technological excellence: a long way to go and an uncertain outcome

A set of stamps issued in Hong Kong in 2005 illustrated the Four Great Inventions (*Si Da Fa Ming*) of ancient China: the compass, papermaking, printing and gunpowder. The theme was taken up again to stunning effect in the opening ceremony of the Beijing Olympics on 8 August 2008, sending a message to the world that scientific creativity was still alive and well in an eternal China. The following month, the Shenzhou 7 manned space mission saw the first space walk by a Chinese "taikonaut," celebrated by Beijing in a mood of euphoria. The Chinese media were quick to point out that China, now a space power, had achieved the feat well before Japan was capable of doing so. But there was another side to the coin, since in a way it also constituted recognition that Japan's pacifism is real. The limits that Tokyo sets on its military budget inevitably affect how much its space industry can do, given the extent to which civilian and military applications are intertwined.

If China is so eager to emphasise its glorious past and current success, it is because it aims to quickly impose itself as a major technological power. That ambition underlies the National Medium- and Long-term Science and Technology Development Plan (2006–2020), published after detailed consultations with the scientific community lasting several years. Beijing intends to develop the capacity for independent innovation in key sectors for the future and ultimately to double the amount of spending on R&D.[16] The surge in financial and human resources devoted to research since 2000 has been commented on widely both in China and abroad, though not always acknowledging the low starting level. Yet it is a good illustration of the highly proactive approach China intends to take in order to become the world's laboratory and not just its workshop. Promising progress appears to have been made in the aviation, railway, information technology and aerospace industries[17] but there is a very long way to go yet before China can reduce its still very heavy reliance on foreign, and especially Japanese, technologies.[18]

Several factors need to be taken into account in order to assess the current state of Chinese scientific and technological research, including financial and human resources, scientific output and patent filings. R&D spending, 69 per cent of which is company-funded, has more than tripled in six years, but it still represents less than 1.4 per cent of GDP against an OECD average of 2.3 per cent, and seems paltry in relation to the Japanese figure of 3.4 per cent.

China aims to achieve a figure of 2.5 per cent, the developed-country average, by 2020, but that looks a very ambitious or even unattainable objective in view of Chinese firms' financial resources. The same gulf between Japan and China exists with regard to researchers: although the number in China has almost doubled in absolute terms since 2000, reaching 1.6 million in 2008 against 0.7 million in Japan and 1.4 million each in the United States and Europe, it is ten times lower in relation to the workforce (1.6 per thousand in China against 11.1 in Japan). The number is likely to rise sharply over the next few years with the arrival of armies of new graduates, swelling at an annual rate of 20 per cent since 2000. The total number of university graduates in 1990 was only 16 million; it is now nearly 70 million, or 5 per cent of the population (though the proportion in Japan is 38 per cent). Another encouraging sign is that engineering and natural sciences are the most popular subjects, representing over 40 per cent of enrolments. The rate is the same in South Korea but is only 20 per cent in Japan and the other developed countries. Chinese researchers already rank third in the world in terms of articles published, almost on a par with Japan;[19] for nanoscience, China is in second place behind the United States but ahead of Japan. In contrast, though China came fourth for patent applications in 2010 with 7.6 per cent of the world total and an increase of 56 per cent on the previous year, the number of patents filed outside China, though rising, remains very small: 4.4 per cent against 34 per cent for Japan. This figure also includes foreign companies, which tend to be quite active in applying for patents. According to the most recent OECD figures, China obtained only 472 triadic patents in 2008 against Japan's 13,446. Although Chinese patent filings in electronics have increased substantially in Europe and the United

States, they still represent only a tenth of Japanese filings because Chinese "high-tech" companies in fact mostly assemble imported components. But rapid progress could be made in this area, one of the priorities in the 15-Year Plan.[20]

These initial results, and the vast resources due to be mobilised, are evidence that China has embarked on its quest to catch up. Yet it continues to rely on foreign technologies, either imported by Chinese companies or used by foreign subsidiaries in China. The same problem arises here as with "Chinese" exports: it is true that China has become the world's leading exporter of high-tech electronic and telecommunication products, but most of them are manufactured by foreign companies. Likewise, when talking about "Chinese R&D," the contribution made by foreign companies is included in overall statistics on resources allocated, filings for patents, etc., even though the foreign share is often preponderant.

The statistics are fragmentary, meaning that any analysis is bound to contain extensive areas of uncertainty; however, the sources of technological innovation on which Chinese industry draws may be divided into four types. The first is the independent R&D of Chinese companies and research centres, like those belonging to the Academy of Sciences and Tsinghua University, and the clusters and incubators that depend on them. This category includes the national champions mentioned earlier, like ZTE and, above all, Huawei. The second is direct purchases of licences from abroad; the annual cost of imported technologies (excluding equipment) is estimated at USD 12 billion. The third source is the acquisition of foreign technologies by buying the companies that own them: examples include Rover, Volvo and IBM's PC division, acquired by Lenovo. The fourth source, and the most important at the present time, is the technological innovation of foreign companies, especially Japanese firms within the "Asian integrated circuit." Technology transfers may form part of the contract with the Chinese partner in joint ventures; otherwise, technology transfers occur in a diffuse way through improvements in the technical skills of the workforce. Some foreign firms are very willing to set up research centres in China in order to use the local potential; there are now around eight hundred such centres, compared with five hundred belonging to Chinese firms. Altogether, foreign companies obtained 50,000 patents in 2008, half the total number granted in the country.[21] The vital contribution made by foreign firms must be taken into account in any assessment of the true potential of Chinese R&D, since apparent advances do not necessarily mean the development of independent innovation capacities and hence a real closing of the technology gap. Domestic technologies, mainly used in traditional sectors and heavy industry, represent only 30 per cent of the country's technological arsenal;[22] the government is well aware of this reliance on other countries and the aim of the 15-Year Plan is specifically to reverse the ratio by 2020. Another weakness is that Chinese R&D remains highly focused on applied research and development: funds allocated to basic research represent only 5 per cent of the total as against 17 per cent for applied research and 78 per cent for development.

Ultimately, according to the specialists, the situation regarding technological progress in Chinese industry remains ambivalent. China is catching up in certain areas with a high international profile such as carmaking, space, shipbuilding and railways (including tilting trains). Renewable energy sources are another fast-growing sector, while Chinese carmakers aim to catch up quickly with their Japanese rivals in the clean car segment. Great strides have been made in applied research: exchanges of researchers with other countries are increasing and research centres belonging to foreign firms are helping to disseminate technological progress throughout China's industrial fabric. But basic research remains rather skimpy and fails to produce genuine innovation, even in priority sectors like space and electronics. The taikonaut's space walk, for example, was a remarkable feat but the rocket was derived from a relatively old Russian model. In semiconductors, as in artificial intelligence, the technological divide that separates Japanese and Chinese firms will be very difficult to bridge. China has a very long way to go before it can even come close to the technological level achieved by Japan, let alone threaten its supremacy. Japan has been at the top of annual innovation rankings for years. The Economist Intelligence Unit[23] points out that Japan's technological supremacy and its world leadership in innovation stem from the golden rule of its industrial strategy: innovate or die. In other words, Japan has no option but to maintain its technological edge. The same report also emphasises the erosion of American positions and highlights the progress made by the Chinese outsider, which has moved up five places in the rankings in two years. However, that rise was from fifty-ninth to fifty-fourth, so China's race to catch up in innovation is going to be a long one. Moreover, the outcome remains uncertain because Japan, the leader of the pack, is stepping up the pace. Yet China is playing for very high stakes: technology is the key to economic supremacy in Asia, which in turn is a precondition for overall leadership in the region. It is an objective that would seem difficult to achieve before 2025–2030.

The ambitions of a major regional and global player

In Samuel Huntington's words, "China's history, culture, traditions, size, economic dynamism, and self image all impel it to assume a hegemonic position in East Asia."[24] For the neorealist John Mearsheimer, China is an example of a nation seeking to establish hegemony in its own region in order subsequently to extend its sphere of domination and ultimately control the entire global system.[25] On that basis, the only thing China lacks in order to assert itself as the only global power in Asia is economic supremacy, for it already has strategic advantages that Japan does not.

CHINA, A GLOBAL POWER IN THE MAKING

An enterprising and "benign" regional player

China's policy in Asia is built around two objectives: to maintain stability in the region, necessary for its own economic expansion, and to increase its influence by allaying fears of a "Chinese threat." The policy has three main strands: stable borders, regional security and economic diplomacy.

Stable borders and territorial integrity

Since its foundation, the People's Republic of China has been involved in territorial conflicts with various neighbours, threatening the regional equilibrium. They include violent tensions with the USSR in the 1960s and wars with India in 1962 and Vietnam in 1979. The move to stabilise borders over the last two or three decades has been important for two reasons, the first symbolic, because it expunges the humiliation of the "unequal treaties" in the nineteenth century, the second strategic, because without border conflicts China can concentrate on growth. It has settled eleven territorial disputes since 1998 and concluded agreements with almost all the countries with which it has borders. But some disagreements over maritime and land frontiers remain, with Japan and India in particular. In the East China Sea, its dispute with Japan (particularly abrasive during the autumn of 2010) concerns sovereignty over the Senkaku/Diaoyutai islands, because their seabed is rich in hydrocarbons and they would occupy a strategic position in the event of a conflict involving Taiwan. In the South China Sea, several countries have laid claim to the tiny Spratly and Paracel island groups, including China and Vietnam, less for their mineral potential than for their strategic position, in this case on a key shipping lane.

The dispute between China and India over Akasi Chin, part of Kashmir, and Arunachal Pradesh is a long way from any solution, given the level of mistrust between the two countries.[26] Memories of defeat in 1962 run deep in India and close cooperation between Beijing and Islamabad is a cause of concern in New Delhi. But closer economic ties have improved diplomatic relations and President Hu Jintao made an official visit to New Delhi in 2006, China-India Friendship Year. China has accepted Indian sovereignty over Sikkim, while in 2003 India recognised China's sovereignty over the "autonomous region" of Tibet.

Deeply scarred by past foreign domination, China is extremely prickly on matters of territorial integrity and sovereignty. The question of Tibet and, to a lesser extent, the unrest in Xinqiang, typify the challenge posed to Beijing by frontier provinces inhabited by ethnic minorities. The government's attitude towards the Dalai Lama reflects the CPC's intransigence towards any wish for cultural or religious autonomy, immediately labelled secessionist. Even more than the loss of Tibet's mineral wealth, the government fears contagion and the loss of its legitimacy in the eyes of the Chinese population as a whole, almost 95 per cent of whom are ethnic Han.

Taiwan remains the cloud on the horizon:[27] in 2005, the PRC Parliament passed an Anti-Secession Act authorising military intervention if Taipei declared independence, a *casus belli* for Beijing. Escalation would have been extremely dangerous because the United States, tied to Taiwan by a security treaty, would not have been able to stand idly by. The greatest danger to regional stability was removed in 2008 with the defeat of President Cheng's Democratic Progressive Party, openly favourable to Taiwan's independence. The election of the Kuomintang, supporters of the status quo like most of Taiwan's population, has already helped to thaw relations with Beijing and enabled the conclusion of major agreements on air links and financial relations. The conclusion of a free-trade agreement, the Economic Cooperation Framework Agreement (ECFA), signed on 29 June 2010, is a major step forward on the economic front. The political status quo means that the "one China" fiction can be maintained and each party is able to accommodate the contradictory interpretation of the claim made on the other side of the Strait: Taipei's "Three No's" are echoed by Beijing's. For Taiwan, they are no to independence, no to unification and no to the use of force; for Beijing, no to Taiwan's independence, no to two Chinas and no to international recognition of Taiwan. Even if the timing and conditions of Taiwan's return to Chinese sovereignty remain uncertain, the principle is sacrosanct in Beijing's eyes, given its vital symbolic importance. After the return of Hong Kong and Macao, Taiwan is the last vestige of a "century of humiliations," because China had to cede sovereignty over the island to Japan after losing the Sino-Japanese war of 1894–95. Fresh tensions could emerge after the presidential elections in Taiwan in 2012, which will also be a presidential election year in the United States and a year in which China's leadership is renewed.

China's active role in regional security

Security in Asia is a prime objective of Chinese diplomacy because it establishes an environment that favours economic growth. That is why China is so active in a sphere that also enables it to consolidate its regional influence. It brings all its weight to bear on the work of the ASEAN Regional Forum (ARF), considering that, as the only Asian country with permanent membership of the UN Security Council, it represents Asia as a whole, and especially emerging Asia, and is thus authorised to exercise a kind of tutelage over the ASEAN countries.

However, China's ambitions come up against the United States' strategic domination of the region and Beijing feels encircled by a mighty American network of military bases and more or less formal alliances spanning the whole of Asia from north to south. In North Asia, the United States has bases in and security treaties with Japan and South Korea; in South-East Asia, it has agreements with Thailand, Singapore and the Philippines; in

South Asia, it has an ambiguous "dual alliance" with Pakistan and India; in Central Asia, it has a military presence in Afghanistan, Kyrgyzstan and Uzbekistan. This tight web is completed by the US security treaty with Taiwan, the deployment of an anti-missile shield and an omnipresent Pacific fleet. Faced with such a powerful array of force, China's diplomatic action focuses on Central Asia and the Korean peninsula.[28]

China's relations with the countries of Central Asia are ambivalent. It covets their abundant resources but fears the spread of Islamism in its frontier provinces. For China, the Shanghai Cooperation Organisation (SCO), whose permanent secretariat is based in Beijing and whose other members are Russia, Kazakhstan, Kyrgyzstan, Uzbekistan and Tajikistan,[29] is a key instrument for economic and strategic cooperation. By giving those countries sustained development support, China hopes to reduce the influence of Islamism and head off the contagion of separatism in its provinces with a Muslim majority. It reaps two other benefits: preferential access to the abundant oil and other mineral resources in the outer reaches and a kind of rampart against American influence in the region. From this standpoint, China's interests coincide with those of Russia, with which it signed a Friendship and Cooperation Treaty in 2001. Trade between the two countries has not yet achieved its full potential, but Russia is China's leading supplier of arms. More importantly, they share the same reservations about America's power policy and the same conception of a multipolar world order under the aegis of the United Nations. Primarily an economic forum, the SCO is not a kind of Central Asian NATO, though the political dimension is not entirely absent: for China and Russia, it is also a means of containing American influence in Central Asia.

The other key arena of Chinese diplomacy is the Korean peninsula. North Korea has proved quite a headache for China, especially since Pyongyang conducted its second nuclear test in

May 2009. However, a pragmatic approach has left Beijing as the only power capable of preserving stability in the peninsula as a whole and of wielding exclusive influence, thanks to its links with each of the two Koreas. Both the South and the North are essential partners for China, the former for its economic development, the latter for its security, since North Korea, acting as a buffer zone against any American invasion from the South, is "the lips that protect the mouth."[30] Beijing's strategy in the peninsula is thus guided by a dual imperative: territorial security, achieved by keeping a friendly government in power in Pyongyang, and economic cooperation with Seoul. Two issues dominate the peninsula's future: reunification and nuclear weapons. On the first issue, the status quo serves the interests of China, which wants neither a reunified country nor a Seoul-dominated confederation. Nor does it want the North Korean regime to collapse; it would rather see a Chinese-style shift towards "market socialism" and international openness. On the second issue, China is the linchpin of the Six-Party Talks:[31] Beijing is pressuring Pyongyang to renounce nuclear weapons but is willing to use its UN veto to prevent its ally's international isolation. China is playing a highly complex diplomatic game, serving several aims: to maintain regional stability, to remain the only nuclear power in the region and to contain America's influence.

A new and predominantly economic regionalism

We saw in Chapter 3 how China's active approach to free-trade agreements in Asia has obliged Japan to make up lost ground in that sphere. Beyond the direct economic benefits, China's policy forms part of a wider framework that some commentators have compared to the old tribute system mentioned in Chapter 1.[32] On that interpretation, China is seeking to restore the old order, based on an asymmetrical relationship: in the heart of the new Asia, it is the responsible and benign partner that ensures stability and prosperity for all, starting with itself. In more modern terminology, the system of such a Sino-centred Asia would be one of "hegemonic stability,"[33] requiring the conjunction of three elements: the dominant power's desire for hegemony, the capacity to exercise it and the willingness of weaker countries to submit to it.[34] The decisions taken by many ASEAN countries in economic and diplomatic matters are already influenced by a form of Chinese patronage. China's attitude during the Asian crisis in 1997 doubtless played a crucial role in this development. Beijing displayed its sense of responsibility at regional level, refraining from devaluing the yuan at a time when several Asian currencies were collapsing. Its stance won Beijing respect and gratitude which more than made up for any temporary loss of competitiveness.

This new Chinese regionalism, the avatar of a tribute system tinged with neo-mercantilism, is also intended to allay the fear of a "Chinese threat" that remains very much alive in some South-East Asian countries whose Muslim or Christian populations display no particular Chinese bent. Speaking in 2004, the Chinese prime minister, Wen Jiabao, had no hesitation in describing China as a "friendly elephant," doubtless a more attractive image in the Asian bestiary than the dragon. At bilateral level, Beijing is lavish with its offers of "strategic partnership" in a spirit of "good neighbourliness and friendly cooperation." This predominantly economic diplomacy, whose aims are to increase trade flows and give China access to the region's natural resources, focuses on free-trade agreements, direct investment and development assistance. Beijing is one of the main donors to the region's poorest countries but differs from OECD countries in not attaching any governance or human rights conditions to its aid. China's economic diplomacy is even more visible at multilateral level. China's cooperation with ASEAN in the ASEAN+1 framework (ASEAN and China) is more advanced than that of Japan or South Korea, and has already culminated in a free-trade area that came into effect in 2010. China is also increasingly asserting its influence in monetary and financial cooperation within the ASEAN+3 framework, and at meetings of the Asian Development Bank (ADB). It is challenging Japan's former position as the leading influence in the two organisations, as could be seen at the ADB meeting in Bali in May 2009 which followed the G20 summit in London in April: China's emergence as a geopolitical force was very much in evidence on both occasions, in Bali as a top-tier regional player, in London as a global power.

The ambition of global power

A highly active regional player, China is using its influence in Asia as a platform from which to consolidate its international stature and gradually assert itself as a major global power. In doing so, it has two key advantages that Japan lacks: permanent membership of the UN Security Council and nuclear weapons. To achieve its ambitions of global power, Beijing is deploying an aggressive diplomacy whose emphasis on the economic element is sometimes inconsistent with its declared multilateralism; at the same time, it is modernising a "purely defensive" army of over two million whose budget has tripled since the start of the decade.

Tensions between multilateralism and bilateral economic diplomacy

China's greater openness to the rest of the world has a dual dimension: economic, through its accession to the WTO in 2001, and political, through its conversion to multilateralism. Like its regional action in Asia, China's proactive global diplomacy has a twin aim: to promote bilateral trade and to contribute to the stability of the global system on a multilateral and multipolar basis. On certain issues, bilateral diplomacy does not sit easily with the multilateralist option asserted elsewhere, but from Beijing's standpoint the absolute priority given to the country's economic growth involves a measure of pragmatism.

The first aim, developing bilateral economic partnerships, is a priority, so that China can secure its supplies of raw materials and diversify its export markets which are over-reliant on Europe and the United States. Several examples illustrate this strategy, such as the extremely rapid development of relations with Africa, with its wealth of natural resources and promising markets for Chinese goods. China became Africa's largest single trading partner in 2009.[35] Trade, which is balanced and even shows a slight surplus in Africa's favour, has soared since the early 2000s and reached USD 127 billion in 2010.

Sub-Saharan Africa is China's second-largest supplier of oil, providing 27 per cent[36] compared with the Middle East's 39 per cent, and the continent's subsoil contains still largely unexploited deposits of mineral resources of strategic value to Beijing. In return, China exports manufactured goods and services, especially in the construction and civil engineering sectors. The success of this trade-led offensive directed at Africa was crowned by the "Beijing Summit" of November 2006, attended by forty-eight African heads of state to celebrate a "strategic partnership" between China and Africa. During the Sharm el Sheikh summit in November 2009, the Chinese prime minister promised debt write-offs and USD 10 billion of new loans for African countries; he even mentioned around a hundred clean-energy projects that China is preparing to set up in Africa.[37]

Latin America provides another example. Trade with China, now its third-largest partner, has increased tenfold since 2001, from USD 13 billion to USD 140 billion, or 5 per cent of China's total trade. The mutual benefits are obvious: China invests in the oil and mining industries, while on the trade front it exports textiles and electronic goods in return for imports of agricultural produce and raw materials such as iron, copper, tin, nickel and oil. Two events in 2008 illustrated the success of Chinese strategy: China replaced the United States as Brazil's largest trading partner and it became the 48th member of the Inter-American Development Bank.

The economic complementarity that lies behind China's success in Africa and Latin America is not shared to the same extent with other partners. Russia, a near neighbour and the world's largest producer of gas and second-largest producer of oil, should be the ideal partner for energy-hungry China, which has recently replaced Japan as the world's second-largest oil importer. Russia is China's closest partner in several areas, especially military equipment, but territorial disputes and Japanese competition for access to Siberian resources have held back any real cooperation in the energy sphere. Russian oil still accounts for only 10 per cent of China's oil imports, though that percentage is likely to jump with the extension of the Siberia-Pacific pipeline to China.

The European Union (EU), unlike Russia, is a major trading partner, and indeed China's biggest: trade with the EU amounted to EUR 395 billion in 2010 (about USD 513 billion), as against USD 457 billion with the United States. However, it remains a minor strategic partner, since China's priorities, by order of importance, are the United States, Asia and the developing world. Despite regular meetings, the EU's reluctance to grant China the status of a market economy remains the stumbling block to finalisation of a framework partnership and cooperation agreement. Two other difficulties weigh on the relationship: the embargo on arms sales and, above all, the EU's trade deficit, which has increased fourfold since 2001 and amounted to EUR 169 billion in 2010. On the trade front, China cleverly plays off the differences between Member States; more broadly, Europe's common foreign and security policy (CFSP) is too recent and too fragile to support sustained strategic relations.[38] For China, the EU therefore represents an enormous market but not a political force to be reckoned with. However, Chinese academics and civil servants are carefully watching how the European model evolves, because from their standpoint it offers food for thought about what a future Asian Community should or should not look like.

Washington is the primary focus of China's bilateral diplomacy and the priority given by Beijing to economic growth imposes a form of partnership with the United States. During his visit to Beijing in November 2009, President Obama hoped, perhaps naively, to "tame" China's leaders with his restrained and conciliatory attitude. It came to nothing and China did not budge on most of the issues raised, such as undervaluation of the yuan, Iran and North Korea. In contrast, Chinese officials were not short of questions about how the reform of the American health system would be paid for, or of reservations about US budgetary and monetary policy, even going so far as to remind their American counterparts about the rules of free-trade. Nevertheless, the relationship between China and the United States is vital for both economies, since they are locked in step: China needs the US market, the US needs Chinese savings deposits. The latter finance American consumers, who in return sustain Chinese growth by buying Chinese goods. The imbalance created by insufficient savings in the US and excessive savings in China causes a huge American trade deficit, which has more than tripled since 2000 to reach USD 273 billion in 2010. It is by far the largest of America's trading partners, representing 42 per cent of the total deficit. Even more serious for American industry, trade with China accounts for 75 per cent of the total deficit in manufactured goods.[39] That is the main bone of contention between the two partners, as had been the case with Japan in the 1980s, and Washington explains the deficit in the same way now as then, namely by the undervaluation of its partner's currency. The trade deficit and undervaluation of the yuan have dominated the regular meetings between senior officials, though during Hillary

Clinton's visit to Beijing in February 2009 these issues took second place to the need for a coordinated response to the global crisis. For the immediate future, the United States needs China's savings and China needs the American market. Each is the other's hostage in a symbiotic relationship illustrated by the "Chinamerica" concept.[40] This interdependence undermines the notion that Beijing may start a currency "war" by deciding to cash in all or some of its US Treasuries.[41] The boomerang effect would be devastating because the fall of the dollar would mean vast losses for China and a rapid appreciation of the yuan, which is precisely what Beijing is seeking to avoid. In a way, China too is a prisoner of the stock of securities it has accumulated and a currency war is just as unlikely as the use of nuclear weapons during the Cold War, the purpose of which was mutual deterrence. However, Beijing will very probably diversify its foreign currency reserves in the future and, above all, continue its efforts to end the hegemony of the dollar.

This offensive against the international financial system is accompanied by a stealthy challenge to American capitalism and the American hyperpower, which reveals the second component of Chinese foreign policy, namely the refusal of American hegemony and a call for multilateralism rooted in insistence on a multipolar world. The Chinese concept of the world order refers to the five principles of peaceful coexistence set out in Sino-Indian agreements in 1954, namely respect for sovereignty and territorial integrity, non-aggression, non-interference, equality and reciprocal advantages, and peaceful coexistence. It was made more explicit recently in the "new security concept" presented at an ASEAN meeting in 1997 and summarised by Chu Shulong, a Tsinghua University professor, in the "Four No's": no hegemonism, no power politics, no arms races and no military alliances.[42] The refusal of unipolarity goes hand in hand with multilateralism but China is a recent convert, concomitant with its integration into the global economy. It is now present in all the multilateral institutions and forums, while its role at the UN has changed profoundly. China is a mainstay of peacekeeping operations and, with twelve missions, is even the most active of the Security Council's permanent members. It feels driven to speak for developing countries in a world run by the developed nations. The de facto replacement of G8 with G20 validates its strategy and offers China a new platform that it has already used masterfully. It has the potential to become a great power, but above all, and unlike Japan, it has a clear vision of the place it wishes to occupy in tomorrow's world.

Yet China's multilateralism is not entirely unambiguous[43] and its foreign policy is subject to a dialectical tension between the priorities of its economic diplomacy and its ambitions as a responsible great power. Africa is a good example. Beijing's successes there result from an astute playing of its hand: a third-world past, solidarity between developing countries and, above all, to the detriment of the Western world, a refusal of any "interference" in the domestic affairs of African countries, whether in the matter of human rights, for example, or the conditions attached to loans. China's vision of international relations reflects its Westphalian view of its own sovereignty and reaches its limits in the corollary concept of non-interference. The mantra of its Asian policy, non-interference, also guides its international action: thus, Beijing has used the concept to shield Sudan, its partner and protégé, from any condemnation over events in Darfur.

Economic partnerships and multilateral cooperation on key issues are thus the twin strands of Chinese foreign policy. However, the frequency with which the government uses words like "harmonious" and "peaceful" in its "smiling diplomacy" should not mask China's underlying determination to assert itself as a major power. It is sufficient to recall the "24-character strategy" attributed to Deng Xiaoping: "Observe calmly; secure our position; cope with affairs calmly; hide our capacities and bide our time; be good at maintaining a low profile; and never claim leadership."[44]

"Bide our time"? The United States is a key economic partner at the moment, but it is American hegemony that will ultimately be challenged.[45] The quest for supremacy in Asia is just a step on the way. But realism will prevail and Beijing's relations with Washington will doubtless be inspired by the maxim of Jiang Zemin, president from 1993 to 2003, taken up by the defence minister Chi Haotian during a visit to his American counterpart in 1996: "Build trust, decrease trouble, develop cooperation and avoid confrontation."

"Develop cooperation"? The opening in 2009 of a regular "economic and strategic dialogue" between the two countries pursues that goal, but there can be no doubt that considerable tension will remain, especially during the difficult post-crisis years.[46] "Avoid confrontation"? Military confrontation is something to be avoided at all costs, unless conflict erupts over Taiwan. A confrontation between two economic superpowers? The time is not yet ripe. Confrontation via an economic alternative? Little by little, in opening skirmishes, Beijing has already initiated that confrontation of economic and political models on certain issues, such as the international role of the dollar, fair representation at the IMF,[47] the causes of the global financial crisis and a questioning of the development models promoted by US-influenced multilateral institutions. It is not a head-on confrontation because China's strategists are familiar with Sun Tzu's dictum that "supreme excellence consists in breaking the enemy's resistance without fighting."[48] However, given the erosion of a "Washington consensus" around monetarist economics and deregulation, a counter-model (albeit still relatively informal) could begin to emerge, a "Beijing consensus"[49] that some economists have regarded with more interest since the crisis highlighted the excesses of financial capitalism.[50] Despite the democratic deficit in China, the power of attraction of this counter-model for the developing world should not be under-estimated, because it has enabled hundreds of millions of people to free themselves from the shackles of extreme poverty in the space of just twenty years or so.

A rapidly modernising army

John Mearsheimer, the theoretician of "offensive realism," described "the most dangerous scenario the United States might face in the early twenty-first century" as one in which China becomes a hegemon in North-East Asia.[51] According to Mearsheimer, that hegemony would arise from a mighty military machine, financed by the dividends of exceptional growth. The conditions would then be met for a head-on confrontation between the two superpowers, with a very uncertain outcome. He concludes with a criticism of America's policy of supporting China's economic development: "A wealthy China would not be a status quo power but an aggressive state determined to achieve regional hegemony ... Although it is certainly in China's interest to be the hegemon in North-East Asia, it is clearly not in America's interest to have that happen."

China's expanding military potential since 2000 seems to confirm the first part of this view. Strong economic growth since the start of the decade has enabled double-digit growth in the defence budget, which has tripled in nine years. It reached 532 billion yuan (USD 78 billion) in 2010, 1.7 per cent of GDP, and is the second-largest in the world. The Pentagon holds these figures to be greatly understated and estimates China's total military-related spending to be over USD 150 billion.[52] Earlier studies by the Rand Corporation and the Stockholm International Peace Research Institute (SIPRI) confirm the under-estimate, albeit on a lesser scale. China points out that its defence spending remains very small compared with the US military budget, whatever the criterion used (absolute value, percentage of GDP or expenditure per capita).

Chinese military doctrine, as developed in successive editions of the defence White Paper, obviously does not correspond to the second part of Mearsheimer's analysis. Defence policy is presented as a dialectical equilibrium between "defensive" and "offensive" strategies. According to the 2006 edition,[53] it is "purely defensive in nature," though in a "military strategy of active defence," China's armed forces are "well prepared for military struggle, with winning local wars ... and enhancing national sovereignty, security and interests of development as [their] objective." Regional war is deemed legitimate when national sovereignty is threatened, whence the 2005 Anti-Secession Act which authorises the use of "non-pacific means" if Taiwan declares independence. Nuclear weapons are for deterrence only and China undertakes never to use them first "under any circumstances."[54] The role of the armed forces (PLA) is to protect the country's security and interests in order to ensure its "peaceful development." In fact, Beijing's defence policy serves three key strategic objectives which reflect its fears about sovereignty and security: opposing any wish for independence on Taiwan's part, preventing the possible emergence of Japan as a real military power with the capability to intervene beyond its borders, and redressing the balance of forces in Asia, currently to the advantage of the United States.

In recent years, China has spent vast amounts of money on modernising an army which, though very large (2.3 million professionals and conscripts), was under-equipped until the early 2000s. The air force and navy have benefited most: based on Pentagon figures,[55] the equipment renewal rate since 2000 has been 24 per cent in the air force, 23 per cent in naval surface forces and 40 per cent in submarine forces, with priority being given to attack submarines. China has the world's largest missile programme: it has built up its arsenal of ballistic and cruise missiles and Washington estimates that over a thousand short-range missiles have been deployed facing Taiwan since the late 1990s.

The next step is to substantially increase the projection capability of a navy, hitherto restricted to coastal defence. Work on building an aircraft carrier is due to start soon, according to officials responsible for the programme,[56] and the Pentagon believes that it could be operational by 2015. The modernisation of China's armed forces relies to a considerable extent on purchases of sophisticated equipment like fighters, submarines and destroyers from Russia, but little by little the technological advances of the PLA's weaponry allow for production under licence and even the autonomous development of some programmes. China has thus become an exporter of conventional weapons, and arms sales exceeded USD 7 billion between 2003 and 2007, with Pakistan accounting for 36 per cent and Sudan for 25 per cent.[57] At the parade on 1 October 2009 to mark the PRC's sixtieth anniversary, all the equipment on display was of Chinese manufacture, including the J-10 fighter, a rival of the US F-16, and the intercontinental DF-31A nuclear missile, capable of hitting targets on American soil. China greatly strengthened its offensive capabilities during the 2000s, especially in nuclear weapons, cybernetics and space, but the time when it could threaten US military might in Asia still looks a long way off. Beijing is happy enough to live with that situation, because from a Chinese standpoint US presence has three advantages: limiting Japan's ability to assert itself as a military power; forestalling any North Korean invasion of South Korea; and protecting sea lanes. The regional and global status quo is therefore in China's interest until it has consolidated its economic power, augmented its military capacity and increased its cultural influence, notably through the 200 or so Confucius Institutes in almost a hundred countries around the world.

CONCLUSION

THE STAND-OFF BETWEEN CHINA AND JAPAN

Paraphrasing classic Chinese precepts on military strategy,[1] the ambivalence of the stand-off between China and Japan could well be summed up in the maxim "Consider your neighbour as both a friend and a rival."

"Consider your neighbour as a friend." China and Japan have been "friends" since the 1978 Peace and Friendship Treaty. They have cooperated with each other in many areas since then, and summit meetings end with a ritual declaration from their leaders about their desire to seek a "mutually beneficial strategic relationship." Consultation and cooperation are likely to increase, as the Japanese prime minister, Yukio Hatoyama, said when he met the Chinese president, Hu Jintao, in New York on 21 September 2009.[2] Prime minister Shinzo Abe's visit to Beijing in late 2006 had thawed diplomatic relations that had deteriorated sharply under the Koizumi government. Since then, state visits and ministerial meetings have multiplied. In addition, in November 2009 the two countries agreed to carry out joint military exercises for emergency operations in response to natural disasters. The importance of this one-off initiative should not be under-estimated as it could expand into a broader arrangement for the preservation of regional security in which there might also be a place for South Korea. A "China-Japan high-level economic dialogue" was created when the Chinese prime minister, Wen Jiabao, visited Tokyo in 2007 and has now become an annual event.[3] Ministerial meetings take place on many other subjects, but the economic aspect remains central in a consultation process designed to make the most of the complementarity between the two economies. However, although relations have undoubtedly become warmer over the last five years, this has not been the spectacular reconciliation heralded by some media sources and mutual mistrust remains. Despite the proliferation of free-trade agreements in the region, none have been concluded between the two dominant economies. It was not until the DPJ came to power in Japan that such an agreement could even be contemplated, and then only on a trilateral basis with South Korea. Asian integration is another area of cooperation, particularly within ASEAN+3, the preferred forum for regional cooperation in economic and financial matters. Chinese and Japanese diplomats also meet in the ASEAN Regional Forum (ARF) on security issues and the East Asia Summit (EAS) on the plan for an Asian Community.

"Consider your neighbour as a rival." Despite all the cooperation and declarations of friendship, the rivalry between the two countries remains a pervasive obsession in both Beijing and Tokyo, as shown by the diplomatic storm that blew up in September 2010, after an apparently minor naval incident near the disputed Senkaku/Diaoyutai islands. Converging economic interests never eclipse mutual mistrust because everything keeps them apart, whether their interpretation of the past, their perception of the present or their vision of the future: memories of unhealed wounds yesterday, the rise of nationalist sentiment today, rival ambitions for tomorrow.

On the first point, conflicting memories of Japan's militaristic past were exacerbated under the Koizumi government and it looks as though the problem will not be easy to overcome. Tokyo believes that it has clearly apologised on several occasions for the suffering inflicted on the peoples of Asia in the 1930s and 40s. China, however, considers that Japan has only been paying lip service and has never expressed the true repentance called for by the atrocities committed, especially the Rape of Nanking. Beijing sees a negationist tendency at work in Japan, not genuine remorse, finding support for its view in the approval of some revisionist school textbooks and the visits made by prime ministers to the Yasukuni shrine, which honours the memory not only of soldiers who died for their country, but also of fourteen Class-A war criminals.

This diametrically opposed reading of history is compounded by the rise of nationalist sentiment on both sides, which goes hand in hand with their respective positioning in the new geopolitical context in Asia: "peaceful rise" for China, aspiration to "normalisation" for Japan. In China, patriotism is replacing the Communist ideology and being used by the government to reinforce its legitimacy. The exaltation of national identity feeds not only on the country's economic and diplomatic success, but also on the residue of its history, a mixture of pride in a civilisation that goes back thousands of years and resentment for past humiliation, most notably at the hands of Japan. Anti-Japanese demonstrations in the spring of 2005 revealed the Chinese people's endemic dislike of their neighbour. As Jean-Luc Domenach put it after a five-year stay in China, "Hatred of the Japanese is almost unanimous in this country. It is fuelled by bad memories, that much is certain, and some truths, [...] but above all by propaganda and ignorance."[4] Japan is also experiencing a resurgence of nationalism. It wishes to enhance its international stature, and "normalisation" of its defence capability is no longer a taboo subject. Public opinion has been traumatised by the long crisis of the 1990s and by the litany of foreign comment on the "decline of Japan." The Japanese aspire to a restoration of national pride, and China's constant carping about the country's militarist past elicits only lassitude or denial. Japan, too, is caught up in a spiral of mistrust and animosity. Anti-Japanese sentiment in Chinese public opinion is mirrored by Japanese hostility towards China.[5] Chinese nationalism, fuelled by success and dislike of Japan, is answered by a strand of unapologetic nationalist sentiment in Japan whose proponents, while very much in the minority, would like to see their country strong enough to counter China's growing influence in Asia.[6] Even more than the weight of history, the two dominant powers are divided by competing ambitions. Their conflictual relationship with the past and antagonistic assertion of national identity are only symptoms. The real issue at stake is the battle for supremacy in Asia, the duel between the region's dominant economy on the one hand and its strategic power on the other, because for the first time in their history China and Japan are both regional powers at the same time.

Three scenarios seem possible for their future relations, against a background of structural rivalry: Japan's unlikely acceptance of future Chinese hegemony, conflict between enemy rivals, or cooperation between partners with complementary assets. The first would correspond to a hierarchical order that has long prevailed in a Sino-centric Asia, and would see China exercising sway over its neighbours—including Japan, in an avatar of the ancient tribute system. The fact that Japan has always refused to submit to Chinese domination in the past opens the way onto the second scenario, according to which confrontation would be inevitable and could result in violent or even armed conflict if their vital interests—territorial integrity or security of supply—were threatened. According to the third scenario, that of cooperation and partnership, the China-Japan tandem would form the cornerstone of an Asian Community, as the Franco-German partnership did for European construction. Unfortunately, the process of coming to terms with the past, which led to reconciliation between France and Germany, has not taken place in China or Japan, making any such partnership between the two countries unlikely. The dark pages of their common history have been shrouded in such a veil of silence that it has not been possible to heal the wounds of the past. As a result, the two countries' destinies are caught up in a dialectic of fascination and resentment that continues to distort their relations. Though its cultural and moral universe still bears the imprint of imperial China,[7] Japan from the outset rejected any dependence on its larger neighbour with its universalist pretensions. On the contrary, it took advantage of China's momentary weakness to invade the country, asserting its own hegemonic ambitions. That invasion and the atrocities committed in its wake remain deeply ingrained in the Chinese psyche to this day. Painful for the nations that Japan oppressed, the scars of that period are also seared on Japanese memories because Japan was the only country to suffer the nuclear holocaust that put an end to its hubristic military adventure. Its difficulty in coming to terms with the suffering it both inflicted on others, and had to bear itself, delays the time when that past, finally acknowledged, can make way for the demands of the present. Without the necessary reconciliation of their people and the political determination of their leaders, the idea of ambitious and resolute cooperation between China and Japan, along the lines of the Franco-German model, therefore seems just as unlikely as the other two scenarios over the next twenty years.

In fact, these three scenarios are too static: they fail to accommodate any element that may affect the course of history or even the possibility that one scenario may shift towards another over time. A two-stage shift, before and after about 2030, seems the most likely. The first stage, during the next twenty years, will see supremacy in Asia shared between the two countries in an unstable and often conflictual configuration. Japan will maintain its technological and financial supremacy, albeit with China increasingly hard on its heels. In turn, China's political and strategic clout will leave its mark on the reordering of the region. Realism will temporarily impose a form of shared leadership on the two dominant powers because that is what will best correspond to their respective advantages. Japan will dominate in the economic and financial sphere, China in the political and strategic sphere, especially where regional security is concerned. This configuration is also the one that will best serve their interests: Japan will have a vital need for Asian consumers to make up for a domestic market shrinking under the effect of demographic decline, while China will have to prove its strategic leadership in the region in order to claim the global-power status it seeks. There are already so many bones of contention between the two countries that any such co-leadership is bound to be conflictual. It will come to an end when China has caught up and overtaken Japan as the region's dominant economy. A second stage will then begin around 2030 with the emergence of a new regional order whose equilibrium will depend on the scope and extent of integration of a hypothetical Asian Community.

This distant prospect is fraught with uncertainty. However, over the period of twenty years or so with which this book is mainly concerned, it seems likely that the two countries will share leadership against a background of rivalry and conflict. This scenario takes into account both the current configuration—Japan's economic supremacy, China's strategic power—and its likely future shape, with the inexorable narrowing of the economic gap between the two countries.

What are the key aspects of the current configuration? Asia has the highest levels of economic growth in the world, while the emergence of a vast middle class is likely to shift the focus of growth towards domestic demand. Economic integration is progressing and cooperation is being extended to embrace public goods such as regional security, the eradication of poverty, the fight against pandemics and environmental protection. The idea of an Asian Community is making headway, even if it will take decades to achieve, given the disparities in the region. During his brief time in office, Yukio Hatoyama appeared on this issue to show a level of political determination previously lacking, taking up the torch of Tagore's pan-Asian dream[8]—shared in other forms by Sun Yat Sen and Mahathir—of an "Asia for Asians."[9] Nonetheless, China ultimately intends to impose itself as the undisputed leader of Asia in both economic and strategic terms. Consequently, it has to displace Japan as the dominant economic power and counter its regional ambitions. Catching up with Japan in the economic sphere and diplomatic activism are the twin strands of China's Asian strategy. However, its ambition for supremacy in Asia is part of a wider quest for global-power status. China has not forgotten that it stood at the pinnacle until the nineteenth century, and in a way the country remains in the grip of a fantasy of a Middle Kingdom around which the rest of the world would revolve. It has a clear vision of the eminent position it wishes to occupy at global level and a sure confidence in the economic, diplomatic and military advantages that will enable it to achieve that goal.

Japan has turned the page on its militarist adventure and no longer sees its future in hegemonic terms. Any desire for domination seems to have vanished since the 1990s, because the moral and economic crisis of that decade stripped the country of the ambitious national project that had previously galvanised its energies and forced it to outdo itself. The greatest threat to Japan now probably lies in its own inability to imagine a future for itself. Perhaps the Asian Community project promoted by the DPJ will breathe new life into what the country needs most: the return of hope. China advances eagerly into the future, Japan drags its feet; China desires, Japan is disenchanted; China is enterprising, Japan defends its vested interests. It is a matter not so much of escapist retraction but rather of greater lucidity about its singular position in Asia, compounded by great uncertainty about its place in the world. Yet Japan fully intends to defend its primacy in Asia as a sort of birthright. To do so, it is counting not only on its economic advantages, especially its prodigious lead in technology, but also on its status as a pacifist democracy and a great civilian power committed to the promotion of public goods.

As can be seen, neither of the two dominant powers fulfils the economic and strategic conditions for undisputed hegemony in the region, because China will take at least another fifteen years to catch up with Japan in terms of industrial efficiency and technological innovation. Until then, leadership is bound to be shared between the two regional powers, albeit in a conflictual way. The division will be made on the basis of their "comparative advantages" in the economic, financial and strategic spheres. Japan's economic and financial supremacy has its roots in, inter alia, the crucial role played by Japanese firms in the "Asian integrated circuit," its bilateral development aid and its involvement in major regional projects, such as the Mekong basin project.[10] More broadly, Tokyo has undisputed authority in matters of environmental protection, energy efficiency and international finance. Beijing's influence is more apparent in regional security matters, even if the United States remains the real strategic power in the region. However, China has a growing role in the economic and financial sphere through its central place in the "Asian integrated circuit" and highly proactive economic diplomacy. The exceptional vigour of China's economy has benefited all its neighbours, and it showed how responsibly it could behave during the Asian crisis of 1997–98. More recently, the effects of its massive stimulus plan have limited the fallout from the crisis in the region.

Shared leadership between China and Japan is already beginning to emerge, though not without tension, in regional cooperation bodies. The most important of these, ASEAN+3, deals mainly with economic integration, though consultation is slowly being extended to other issues, such as rural development, the eradication of poverty, the management of natural disasters and women's rights. South Korea has succeeded in taking a special place in this arrangement: as a developed economy and OECD member but a medium-sized power, it has a moderating role and acts skilfully as an intermediary between its two larger neighbours. The three countries have agreed to hold an annual trilateral summit, the first of which took place in December 2008. It is to be hoped that South Korea, in its role as moderator, will be able to withstand the pressures that will inevitably arise from Sino-Japanese co-leadership of Asia.

That shared leadership is bound to be conflictual because mistrust between the co-leaders runs deep and their aims are incompatible. China's objective is supremacy in Asia, a necessary precondition for its global ambitions. At the same time, Japan will most certainly refuse to become a sort of satellite or protectorate in a relationship that would make it a de facto vassal of the Chinese suzerain.

The implicit distribution of roles imposed by the current balance of forces has already been challenged, with China making moves in the economic and financial sphere and Japan doing likewise in the field of security, expanded to "human security." Chinese advances in the financial arena over the last two years are a particularly enlightening example. At regional level, Beijing is challenging Tokyo's leadership in financial stabilisation mechanisms, while at global level it has attacked the dollar's monopoly by proposing that the international currency should ultimately be indexed to a basket of currencies. In addition to these incursions into what had hitherto been jealously guarded hunting grounds, tensions could well flare up in two areas in particular. The shape of the regional architecture and access to natural resources will doubtless be the two major stumbling blocks to continuing the Chinese and Japanese co-leadership.

The two countries have opposing views on the subject of regional construction. China believes its scope should be that of ASEAN+3, whereas Japan is campaigning for ASEAN+6, which includes Australia, India and New Zealand. Japan won the first round by gaining approval of ASEAN+6 as the perimeter for the annual East Asia Summit, but that does not prejudge what the final shape of a putative East Asian Community might be. The cause of the disagreement is obvious. China prefers ASEAN+3, where it wields more influence; Japan prefers ASEAN+6 because the close links it has forged with Australia, New Zealand and, latterly, India would enable it to establish an "arc of democracy" acting as a rampart against Chinese ambitions. Access to resources, vital for both countries, is another source of conflict. They are already involved in two disputes over hydrocarbons. As well as a territorial dispute over the Senkaku/Diaoyutai islands, they disagree about their maritime frontiers and hence the ownership of fish stocks or energy sources in certain zones, especially the oil and gas fields in the East China Sea. They had already been engaged, via Russia, in a long-running confrontation over the route of the pipeline taking Siberian oil to the Asia Pacific region. Concerning minerals, China indicated in September 2009 that it could limit its global exports of rare-earth metals, over which it has a virtual monopoly since it accounts for 90 per cent of global output. These minerals are essential in many areas of high technology. Any such step would asphyxiate some Japanese manufacturers and could herald a strangulation strategy that would pose a particular threat to Japan's technological supremacy.

Japan's key advantage, and the one that justifies the sharing of leadership in Asia, is its technological lead coupled with unrivalled industrial efficiency. That lead will be eroded over time and China will probably have made up much of the lag within fifteen to twenty years. Yet income per capita will still be three or four times lower than in Japan because productivity will remain low, not least because of the size of the agricultural sector. But with a workforce thirteen times larger, China's economy could be four times as big as Japan's.[11] Beijing will then be in a position to impose both its economic and its political dominance on the rest of Asia, albeit in the form of a friendly and "benign" partnership.

Depending on the progress of the Asian Community project, two hypotheses can be envisaged for the second sequence that would unfold from 2030 onwards. If the project resulted in a community comprising the current participants in the EAS,[12] Japan would doubtless find its place as part of a triumvirate with China and India. The size of India's population and its strategic clout would limit China's influence and the Community would be inspired by the democratic values that most of its members share. If, on the contrary, the Community comprised only ASEAN+3, it would be entirely under the sway of a China able to impose its demographic, economic and strategic power on the region in a form of "hegemonic stability." It seems inconceivable, in this Sino-centred Asia, that Japan would accept an allegiance to China that it has refused for centuries:[13] the history of their tortured relationship could not end with the dishonour of a submission that would write an intolerable epilogue to the five-step sequence described in Chapter 1 (kinship, emancipation, betrayal, aggression, recognition). But the fact of avoiding a confrontation that it would neither want nor be able to meet does not mean that Japan would succumb to the temptation of decline. It would doubtless find a new position for itself, combining economic power, financial wealth, strong conventional defence and international influence through the promotion of global public goods. In a nutshell, Japan would become a kind of Asian Switzerland, prosperous and pacifist. Rather than becoming a satellite, Japan would leave China's orbit and spin off on its own path. The prospects for an Asian Community are distant, given the disparities in the region and the reluctance of former colonies to cede any of their sovereignty. Asia's future in the next two decades will therefore provisionally be dominated by Sino-Japanese co-leadership, accepted pragmatically, but subject to the strong pressures of intense competition.

That stand-off already heralds another. China's rivalry with Japan, however fierce, is in a way oblique. In fact, the decisive duel on which Beijing will one day embark will be a head-to-head confrontation with the United States, parallel to the rise of a Sino-centred Asia and the relative decline of an American-centred West. A superpower in the making, China ultimately intends to challenge American hegemony and to influence the world order in a dialogue of equals with the United States. After Japanese supremacy, it is the American hegemon that Beijing will seek to challenge, first in Asia as a result of the weakening of its Japanese ally, then in the rest of the world as China closes the considerable power gap in relation to the United States. The year 2009 marked a turning point in China's assertion of its global ambitions. A self-confident and determined Chinese president dominated the London G20 summit in April 2009. A few days earlier, bolstered by the Chinese economy's capacity to withstand the global crisis, Beijing had even challenged the hegemony of the dollar. It had also made a veiled criticism of the American disorders behind the global crisis and called for representation at the IMF in keeping with its economic importance.

At the same time, the Chinese and American presidents decided to establish a regular economic and strategic dialogue. Some commentators regarded this as a sign that Beijing saw itself as a key dialogue partner for the US and that their G2 would act as a sort of governing council for a new world order. It is true that Beijing's approval is now essential on major international issues, and that the United States must reckon with China. Their cooperation bore fruit during the global crisis, but their confrontation also led to the quasi-failure of the Copenhagen climate conference in December 2009. President Obama had conceded the real state of affairs in July 2009, when he declared at the opening of the first "economic and strategic dialogue" that "the relationship between the United States and China will define the twenty-first century." Does that mean that a Sino-American G2 will henceforth jointly manage the world's affairs? China's position is unambiguous: it does not share that bipolar vision and is not inclined to assume such responsibilities. The Chinese prime minister, Wen Jiabao, was quite clear on the matter at the China-EU summit in Prague on 20 May 2009: "Some say that world affairs will be managed solely by China and the United States. I think that view is baseless and wrong ... Multipolarisation and multilateralism represent the larger trend and the will of the people... China will never seek hegemony."[14]

To imagine a Sino-American G2 along those lines is also to forget the gulf that still separates China and US hyperpower in both economic and military terms. The scenario of a *pax sinica* replacing the *pax americana* likewise seems very remote, even if it is consistent with the tide of history. But Chinese strategists are already whispering to emerging countries about an outline "Beijing consensus" that would replace a moribund "Washington consensus." The "helmsmen" who have succeeded Mao are well aware of the price of time, but they harbour the same dream as he did: to outstrip the United States and make China the new centre of the world.

NOTES

INTRODUCTION

1. Robert Guillain, *Japon Troisième Grand*, Paris: Le Seuil, 1969; translated into English by Patrick O'Brian as *The Japanese Challenge*, Philadelphia: Lippincott, 1970.
2. Until the early nineteenth century, Asia represented approximately 60 per cent of the global economy. See Angus Maddison, *The World Economy: A Millennial Perspective*, Paris: OECD, 2001.
3. The arguments about states' power, especially those that divide the neo-realist school of Waltz, Gilpin and Mearsheimer (uni-, bi- or multipolar, the regional or global nature of hegemony, etc.) go beyond the scope of this book.
4. Paul Kennedy, *The Rise and Fall of the Great Powers*, New York: Vintage Books, 1989, p. XV (our emphasis).

1. GENEALOGIES OF TWO ECONOMIC GIANTS

1. In 2010, China's nominal GDP reached USD 5,879 billion against USD 5,474 billion for Japan.
2. Martin Ravallion, "Are There Lessons for Africa from China's Success against Poverty?," *World Bank Working Paper 4463*, 2008. With a poverty threshold of two dollars a day, the figure rises to 29 per cent (World Bank, *An East Asian Renaissance*, 2007).
3. Jean-Baptiste du Halde, *Description géographique, historique, chronologique, politique et physique de l'empire de la Chine et de la Tartarie chinoise*, Paris: Lemercier, 1735, Vol. II, p. 169.
4. Adam Smith, *An Inquiry into the Nature and Causes of the Wealth of Nations*, London: W. Strathan & T. Cadeli, 1776, Book One, Chapter 11, 1776.
5. Angus Maddison, *Chinese Economic Performance in the Long Run, 960–2030*, Paris: OECD, 2007. (GDP is expressed in purchasing power parity.

regional base).

6. The four newly industrialised Asian countries: South Korea, Hong Kong, Singapore and Taiwan.

7. Malaysia, Thailand, Indonesia, the Philippines and Brunei.

8. Life expectancy at birth rose from 40 to 65 years between 1955 and 1980. See Gérard Calot, *Population*, 39 (6), 1984, p. 1058.

9. The acute phase of the Cultural Revolution lasted from 1966 to 1969 but the power struggle between rival factions continued until Mao's death in 1976.

10. See World Bank, *Working Paper 4729*, September 2008.

11. In his posthumous memoirs, Zhao Ziyang, former prime minister and general secretary of the Chinese Communist Party, disputes the central role in the reforms attributed to Deng. See Zhao Ziyang, *Prisoner of the State*, New York: Simon & Schuster, 2009.

12. As demonstrated by his intransigent reaction to the Tiananmen Square events in 1989.

13. Within the Party apparatus, he drew on the concept of the "Four Modernisations" (agriculture, industry, science and technology, defence) formulated by Zhou Enlai in 1975 and violently condemned at the time by Mao.

14. *Time*, 4 November 1985.

15. See Barry Naughton, *The Chinese Economy: Transitions and Growth*, Cambridge: MIT Press, 2007.

16. The urbanisation rate, only 19.6 per cent in 1980, is now 45 per cent and is likely to reach 60 per cent by 2030. See UN Population Division, *World Urbanisation Prospects: The 2007 Revision*.

17. The "private" sector includes collective enterprises under the aegis of local authorities, especially township and village enterprises. See Wei Zou, "The Changing Face of Rural Enterprises," *China Perspectives*, no. 50, Nov.-Dec. 2003.

18. Foreign shareholdings were initially limited to 25 per cent.

19. And USD 108 billion in 2008. See UNCTAD, *World Investment Report 2009*.

20. Tariffs were slashed after China became a member of the WTO in 2001.

21. On the influence of Confucianism today, see Daniel A. Bell, *China's New Confucianism*, Princeton: Princeton University Press, 2008.

22. The similarity between this motto and China's "A rich and powerful country" (*fuqiang*) is due to their shared origin in the chronicles of the Fighting Kingdoms (5th–3rd centuries BCE).

23. In 1878, 80 per cent of the population worked on the land and produced two thirds of the country's national income. At the time the country had

only 35 million inhabitants, compared with 73 million in 1940 and 127 million now.

24. The Communist forces' victory in China in 1948 was followed by the start of the Korean War in 1950.

25. Hubert Brochier, *Le miracle économique japonais*, Paris: Calmann-Lévy, 1965.

26. On this period, see Christian Sautter's authoritative book *Japon, le prix de la puissance*, Paris: Seuil, 1973.

27. For further details, see Claude Meyer, *La puissance financière du Japon*, Paris: Economica, 1996, pref. Christian Sautter, Chapters 3 and 6.

28. See Chalmers A. Johnson, *Japan: Who Governs? The Rise of the Developmental State*, New York: Norton, 1995.

29. He was elected by the LDP base and not, as had previously been the practice, after back-room deals between party factions.

30. The reforms also accentuated the two-tier labour market: the proportion of non-regular workers (the "floating workforce") rose from 20 per cent in the 1990s to 34 per cent in 2008. See OECD, *Economic Survey of Japan 2009*.

31. On the respective roles of state and private sector capitalism in China's success, see Yasheng Huang, *Capitalism with Chinese Characteristics: Entrepreneurship and the State*, Cambridge: Cambridge University Press, 2008 and "Private Ownership: The Real Source of China's Economic Miracle," *McKinsey Quarterly*, December 2008.

32. The system was probably introduced under the Han dynasty (206 BCE to 220 CE).

33. "… the fixedness of a character which recurs perpetually, takes the place of what we should call truly historical…. The Substantial … rules therefore, not as the moral disposition of the Subject, but as the despotism of the Sovereign." G.W.F. Hegel, *The Philosophy of History*, trans. J. Sibree, London: George Bell & Sons, 1857.

34. See Seiichi Iwao (ed.), *Dictionnaire historique du Japon*, Tokyo/Paris: Maison franco-japonaise/Maisonneuve & Larose, 2002, p. 302, article "Chôko-bôeki."

35. "Datsu-A Ron" ("Goodbye Asia"), *Jiji Shinpō*, 16 March 1885.

36. In 1940, militarist Japan put a theoretical gloss on its expansionism by developing the concept of a "Greater East Asia Co-Prosperity Sphere."

2. MIGHTY BUT VULNERABLE

1. Two-thirds of foreign capital is of Asian origin. Of this, 40 per cent comes from Hong Kong (including investments by Chinese and foreign firms through their Hong Kong subsidiaries), 8 per cent from Japan and 6 per

cent from Taiwan. The share of the United States and the EU is around 8 per cent, the same as Japan.

2. USD 78 billion in 2009, or 3.2 per cent of total investment.

3. On the role of Asian FDI in the shift from a self-sufficient continental China to a trading maritime Asia, see François Gipouloux's Braudelian analysis in *La Méditerranée asiatique*, Paris: CNRS Editions, 2009.

4. Source: OICA. Japan was the world's leading producer in 2008. China was second, ahead of Germany for cars and ahead of the United States in terms of the total number of vehicles, including commercial vehicles.

5. Ford's sale of AB Volvo's automobile division to Geely was confirmed in December 2009 and concluded in March 2010 for USD 1.8 billion (Ford had paid USD 6.4 billion for Volvo in 1999).

6. In 2010, exports amounted to USD 1.58 trillion and generated a trade surplus of USD 183 billion. This surplus represented 3 per cent of GDP against 7 per cent in 2008, an exceptional level for an emerging country. If services are included, China is the third-largest exporter behind the United States and Germany with a market share of 8 per cent.

7. The hourly wage in manufacturing in 2006 was USD 1.35 in China compared with USD 24 in OECD countries, USD 6.50 in Taiwan, USD 3.20 in Brazil and USD 2.50 in Mexico (national sources).

8. At the same time the share of textiles and clothing has fallen from 25 to 14 per cent of the total while doubling from 13 to 27 per cent of the global market. The plant and equipment sector has a market share of 15 per cent.

9. See *China Monthly Statistics* (Chinese statistics differ from those of its partners, especially for trade with Hong Kong).

10. The economies of Singapore, Brunei, Hong Kong and Malaysia are particular cases on account of their size and externally-oriented structure.

11. However, Japan remains the world's largest creditor nation with net assets of USD 2.8 trillion at end-2009 and the United States the world's largest debtor nation with net liabilities of more than USD 3.5 trillion.

12. In June 2005, the China National Offshore Oil Corporation (CNOOC) made a USD 18 billion takeover bid for the American oil company, Unocal. The bid was withdrawn on account of a threatened block by the American government on national security grounds.

13. Like Morgan Stanley and Barclays. See *McKinsey Quarterly*, "Global Investment Strategies for China's Financial Institutions," June 2008.

14. China, with 20 per cent of the world's population, currently accounts for only 3 per cent of its consumption.

15. See Jianwu He and Louis Kuijs, "Rebalancing China's Economy: Modelling a Policy Package," *World Bank China Research Paper No. 7*, Sept. 2007.

16. Now 37 per cent, compared with 58 per cent in Japan.
17. Chinese employment statistics are notoriously unreliable. See OECD, *Economic Survey of China 2005*, pp. 83 et seq.; and Judith Banister, "Manufacturing employment in China," *Monthly Labor Review*, July 2005.
18. However, the reservoir of young, unskilled workers in the rural population is likely to run dry in ten years or so.
19. Including 18 million in vocational schools.
20. Seventy-two per cent of children attend secondary school, 20 per cent go on to higher education and only 10 per cent of the population are illiterate (the corresponding figures for India are 53 per cent, 12 per cent and 38 per cent).
21. "Getting the Numbers Right: International Engineering Education in the United States, China and India." *Journal of Engineering Education*, 97(1), January 2008, p. 16, Fig. 1.
22. Which raises the question of a possible outflow of labour in the future. 750,000 migrants already work in Asia, Africa and the Middle East, not only for Chinese firms but also for local companies using Chinese recruitment agencies, legal or not. See *New York Times*, 20 December 2009.
23. This pattern was then extended to comparative analyses of several sectors and countries with a fourth phase of relocation.
24. On the strategic importance of this sector, see Bernadette Bensaude-Vincent, "Nanotechnologies: une révolution annoncée," *Etudes*, Dec. 2009.
25. Relocated production accounted for 6 per cent of total output in 1990 and now runs at barely 19 per cent.
26. This crucial point will be considered in more detail in Chapter 4.
27. See Asian Development Bank, http://aric.adb.org/10.php.
28. See METI, *Summary of the 37th Survey on Overseas Business Activities*, 2008, p. 10 and JETRO, *White Paper 2008*, p. 214.
29. The yen almost doubled in value after the Plaza Accords in September 1985, causing the government to slash interest rates.
30. The Gini index, which measures income inequality on a rising scale from 0 to 1, was 0.28 in 1980 and is currently 0.47, compared with 0.33 in France and 0.38 in Japan. Comparison is difficult, however, because the sources (UN, CIA, etc.) use the most recent available national data, which may sometimes not be very recent at all.
31. CRS Report for Congress, *Social Unrest in China*, 2006, p. 10.
32. See Yu Jianrong, "Social Conflict in Rural China," *China Security*, 3 (2), 2007, pp. 2–17.
33. Source: IEA Statistics, *CO$_2$ Emissions from Fuel Combustion 2009*. However, the United States remains the biggest emitter per inhabitant, with a level four times higher than China.
34. Interview with Pan Yue, *Der Spiegel*, 3 July 2005.

35. Some sources, disputed by China, give a figure of 750,000 deaths a year linked to pollution. See USCC, *2008 Annual Report*, Washington DC, 2009, p. 194, note 82.

36. World Bank & SEPA, *Cost of Pollution in China*, 2007.

37. See State Council of the People's Republic of China, *Environmental Protection in China*, Beijing, June 2006, Chapter 9.

38. Kenneth Lieberthal and Michel Oksenberg, *Policy Making in China: Leaders, Structures and Processes*, Princeton: Princeton University Press, 1988.

39. McKinsey & Co., *Pathways to a Low-Carbon Economy*, 2009.

40. See China Greentech Initiative, *China Greentech Report 2009*. http://www.chinagreentech.com/report.

41. Carbon intensity measures the quantity of CO_2 emitted per unit of GDP. The Chinese proposal does not therefore guarantee a reduction of emissions in absolute terms if growth remains strong.

42. The EU proposed a 20 per cent reduction in relation to 1990, the benchmark year for the Kyoto Protocol.

43. The terms and implementation of the agreement are not due to be reviewed until 2016.

44. Source: Xinhua press agency, 29 February 2009.

45. UN, *World Population Prospects: The 2008 Revision*.

46. China is already one of the world's leading producers of wind and solar power, concentrated respectively in Mongolia and Shandong. For wind power it is now in second place behind the United States, with capacity having doubled each year since 2005. See Centre d'Analyse Stratégique, *Le pari de l'éolien*, Nov. 2009, p. 33 ff. It is also rapidly expanding the strategic and heavily subsidised clean car sector.

47. In 2009, crude oil imports represented 10 per cent of total world imports and 51 per cent of China's needs. Those needs increased by 81 per cent between 2000 and 2009, compared with 10 per cent for the world as a whole (see *BP Statistical Review of World Energy*, June 2010, and IEA, *Key World Energy Statistics 2010*).

48. See *Journal of Energy Security*, June 2009. In August 2009, Sinopec bought the Canadian oil company Addax, which owns reserves in Nigeria, Gabon and Iraq, for USD 7.5 billion.

49. See Claude Meyer, "Should China Revalue its Currency? Lessons from the Japanese Experience," GEM-Sciences Po, *Policy Brief*, April 2008.

50. See Jeffrey A. Frankel, "New Estimation of China's Exchange Rate Regime," *NBER Working Paper 14700*, February 2009. Since the reform in July 2005, the yuan has been linked not to the dollar but to a basket of currencies, at least in theory.

51. Around 20 per cent on a Real Effective Exchange Rate (REER) basis. See

also William R. Cline and John Williamson, "Estimates of Fundamental Equilibrium Exchange Rates," *Policy Brief 10–15*, Peterson Institute for International Economics (IIE), May 2010, and "Currency Wars?," *Policy Brief 10–16*, IIE, November 2010.

52. See US Department of Commerce—Bureau of Economy Analysis website. http://www.bea.gov/interactive.htm

53. If the yuan were allowed to float freely, its effective exchange rate could double by 2020 as a result of productivity gains and hence reach its purchasing power parity.

54. See Zhao Ziyang, *Prisoner of the State.*

55. Benoît Vermander, *Chine brune ou Chine verte? Les dilemmes de l'Etat-parti*, Paris: Presses de Sciences Po, 2007, pp. 13–20.

56. Jean-Luc Domenach, *La Chine m'inquiète*, Paris: Perrin, 2008, p. 115.

57. Seventy-three per cent of firms say that they make "informal" payments to civil servants, compared with 54 per cent for Asia as a whole and 13 per cent for the OECD countries. See World Bank, *Enterprise Survey*, 2006.

58. President from 1993 to 2003.

59. Chinese vice-president Xi Jinping's promotion on 19 October 2010 and his nomination as vice-chairman of the powerful Central Military Commission of the ruling Communist Party are, however, clear indications that he will succeed the Chinese president and party chief, Hu Jintao, in 2012.

60. UN, *World Population Prospects: The 2008 Revision.* The number of workers per retiree could thus fall from 2.9 in 2010 to 1.9 in 2030 and 1.4 in 2050.

61. And taking account of advances in robotics, which some studies suggest could make up for the loss of 3 million workers by 2025.

62. IMF, *World Economic Outlook Database*, October 2010.

63. OECD, *Government at a Glance*, 2009.

64. Japan is the world's third-largest producer of nuclear power behind the United States and France. China's primary energy sources are coal (64 per cent), oil (18 per cent) and other (18 per cent). Nuclear power accounts for 0.8 per cent. See IEA, *Key World Energy Statistics 2010.*

65. The amount of energy required per unit of GDP.

66. China is estimated to have lost USD 3 billion on subprimes and Japan USD 9 billion. Their enormous claims on Fannie Mae and Freddie Mac (USD 396 billion for China, USD 228 billion for Japan) were saved by the two agencies' nationalisation.

67. Especially in the steel, aluminium, cement, chemicals, oil refining and wind power sectors. See EU Chamber of Commerce in China, *Overcapacity in China*, 26 November 2009.

68. METI, *White Paper on International Economy and Trade 2009*, Summary.
69. In October 2009, retail prices had fallen by 2.2 per cent over one year and the yen had risen by 30 per cent since July 2008.
70. Loans and guarantees representing 22.5 per cent of GDP should be added to these five stimulus plans.
71. In particular, the promise to boost household consumption by means of a budget stimulus equivalent to about 2.25 per cent of GDP a year from 2010 to 2014.
72. See Hugh Patrick, "Japan's Deep Recession and Prolonged Recovery," Center on Japanese Economy and Business, Columbia Business School, 14 Sept. 2009.

3. JAPAN, AN ECONOMIC LEADER LOOKING FOR NORMALISATION

1. Ichiro Ozawa, the DPJ's former strongman, already said in his *Blueprint for a New Japan* (1993) that Japan should become an "ordinary" country, controlling its own destiny and defending its own interests.
2. See Herodotus, *Œuvres complètes—L'enquête*, Paris: Gallimard, Bibliothèque de la Pléiade, 1971, p. 53.
3. China, Japan, South Korea, Hong Kong, Taiwan and the ten ASEAN countries.
4. ASEAN, the Association of South-East Asian Nations, was created in 1967 by Indonesia, Malaysia, the Philippines, Singapore and Thailand to protect themselves against the spread of Communism through economic development. Since joined by Brunei, Myanmar, Cambodia, Laos and Vietnam, its prevailing principle has been mutual non-interference, the cornerstone of the "ASEAN spirit."
5. North American Free-Trade Agreement, a free-trade area between Canada, Mexico and the United States.
6. For the automobile industry, see Herbert Dieter, "Transnational Production Networks in the Automobile Industry," *Notre Europe*, June 2007, pp. 45 et seq.
7. Newly Industrialised Asian Countries (Dragons and Tigers).
8. In sectors like electronics, the first stage is often subdivided: Japan and the Dragons produce components that are then exported to the Tigers for intermediate assembly.
9. This is part of a wider movement resulting from the lack of progress in the Doha Round. On 2 December 2009, twenty-two developing countries, seven of them from Asia, concluded a "South-South" agreement to reduce customs tariffs.

10. See Asia Regional Integration Center website. http://aric.adb.org. China is party to twenty-three of the agreements, nineteen of them within the region, and Japan to nineteen, fifteen of them within the region.

11. JETRO, *White Paper 2007*, p. 132. The extra growth would amount to 1 per cent for Japan, 1.7 per cent for China and 2.3 per cent for ASEAN.

12. See WTO, *International Trade Statistics 2009*. However, it should be remembered that foreign firms account for over half of Chinese exports.

13. China, South Korea and Japan account for 85 per cent of East Asian GDP.

14. A term coined in 1989 by John Williamson, who disputes the subsequent extensive interpretation whereby it is taken to mean excessive budgetary austerity and deregulation. See *A Short History of the Washington Consensus*, Institute for International Economics, 2004.

15. For Paul Krugman, Asia's growth was due solely to the intensity of investment and labour. He does not believe in an "Asian miracle." See "The Myth of Asia's Miracle," *Foreign Affairs*, 73 (6), 1994, pp. 62–78.

16. Emerging Asian bond markets (i.e. excluding Japan) represent a mere 6 per cent of the world total, whereas currency reserves account for 35 per cent and stock market capitalisation for 16 per cent.

17. The common currency project was on prime minister Hatoyama's roadmap for an Asian Community along the lines of the European model, as he recalled at the summit between China, South Korea and Japan on 10 October 2009. See "My political philosophy," *Voice*, Sept. 2009.

18. European Currency Unit.

19. For Chinese viewpoints on this issue, see Jean François Di Meglio, "Vers l'internationalisation du renminbi?" *China Analysis*, 25, Asia Centre, 2009.

20. In March 2009, China proposed using IMF Special Drawing Rights (SDR) as an international currency instead of the US dollar.

21. The term "Cool Japan" has become a promotional device. See Douglas McGray, "Japan's Gross National Cool," *Foreign Policy*, May 2002 and *Critique internationale*, 39, 2008/1, Presses de Sciences Po.

22. MITI, *Quarterly Survey of Overseas Subsidiaries*, 23 March 2009.

23. See Dieter Ernst, "Fragmentation, Modularization and System Integration—Asia's New Position in Global Innovation Networks," http://www.allacademic.com/meta/p70501_index.html

24. Exports to Asian subsidiaries account for about 13 per cent of Japan's total exports. See MITI, *Summary of the 37th Survey on Overseas Business Activities*, 2008.

25. China's international currency reserves are almost three times as much as Japan's, but this does not take account of its debt.

26. Japan was in fifth place in the world ranking in 2009 with USD 9.5 billion.

27. Joseph Nye, *Soft Power: The Means to Success in World Politics*, New York: Public Affairs, 2004. Soft power is defined as the power of influence or persuasion exerted on other countries without threat or the use of force.

28. See Chi Ung Kwan, "The Rise of China and Asia's Flying-Geese Pattern of Economic Development," NRI Papers, 52, August 2002.

29. The value of Chinese exports (excluding Hong Kong) more than quadrupled between 2002 and 2008, rising from USD 325 billion to over USD 1.4 trillion.

30. Most high-technology products are merely assembled in China from imported components, generating relatively little added-value.

31. European Commission, *Global Europe—EU Performance in the Global Economy*, Oct. 2008. Japan's share of the US market fell by 8 points while China's rose by 10 points.

32. Well ahead of the United States (18 per cent), South Korea (9 per cent), Germany (8 per cent) and France (3 per cent). See *China Statistical Yearbook 2008*, Tables 21–49.

33. Though the possibility of a free-trade agreement between China, Japan and South Korea was raised at a trilateral summit in October 2009.

34. Japanese firms fear Chinese competition in emerging countries more than competition from South Korean, American or European firms. See MITI, *White Paper on International Economy and Trade 2008*, Section 3.

35. Named after the then prime minister, who signed the San Francisco Treaty and the Security Treaty.

36. Another reason for the change in attitude lay in Japan's humiliation in the first Gulf war. Tokyo had been subject to harsh criticism from the allies for writing cheques instead of getting involved on the ground, even if only in support operations.

37. The achievements of the forum, which celebrated its twentieth anniversary in 2009, have been rather disappointing, to the point where some derisively claim that the acronym stands for "A Place to Enjoy Coffee."

38. See William Tow et al., *Asia-Pacific Security. US, Australia and Japan and the New Security Triangle*, London: Routledge, 2008.

39. Especially in joint naval exercises for maritime security, an essential issue for Japan since 80 per cent of its oil supplies pass through the Bay of Bengal and the Malacca Straits.

40. See Claude Meyer, "Les relations Inde-Japon: vers un partenariat global?" in Jean-Luc Racine (ed.), *L'Inde et l'Asie. Nouveaux équilibres, nouvel ordre mondial*, Paris: CNRS Editions, 2009, pp. 153–77.

41. See Peter J. Katzenstein, "Japan in the American Imperium: Rethinking Security," *The Asia-Pacific Journal—Japan Focus*, Oct. 2008.

42. In the 2004 Japanese defence White Paper, China had replaced Russia as a potential threat.

43. Literally "… situations in areas surrounding Japan that will have an important influence on Japan's … security." Ratification by parliament ran into fierce opposition and was not completed until 1999.

44. According to informations published by *Japan Today* and *Kyodo News*, China's defence budget for 2010 is actually 1.5 times greater than the amount announced. See *Japan Today*, 8 July 2010. The Chinese defence ministry immediately rejected the reports. See *China Daily*, 10 July 2010.

45. Raymond Aron, *Peace and War*, London: Weidenfeld & Nicolson, 1966.

46. The Treaty was replaced in 1960 by the Mutual Cooperation and Security Treaty, the cornerstone of the US-Japan alliance, whose 50th anniversary the two countries celebrated in 2010.

47. Emeritus professor at the University of California at Berkeley.

48. These three "anti-nuclear" principles were framed in 1967.

49. Japan has since taken part in a dozen peacekeeping operations in Asia, Africa and the Middle East. See Ministry of Defence, *White Book 2008*, p. 283.

50. Laws on terrorism and the state of emergency were passed in 2001 and 2003, allowing the Japanese navy to be sent to the Indian Ocean to give logistical support to operations in Afghanistan.

51. The issue resurfaces periodically, especially each time North Korea performs a nuclear test.

52. See "My Political Philosophy."

53. The US Fifth Air Force and Seventh Fleet are based in Japan, where they serve as a sort of US aircraft carrier in Asia. Over 50,000 US troops are stationed on Japanese soil, including in Okinawa, where their presence is most controversial.

54. Are we seeing a return to cheque-book diplomacy? From 2010, Tokyo will support the allied effort in Afghanistan through a five-year USD 5 billion contribution in place of the logistical support previously provided by the Japanese navy.

55. A joint committee meets at regular intervals to update interpretation of the Treaty. The agreement of 29 October 2005 states that "the US will maintain forward-deployed forces, and augment them as needed, for the defence of Japan as well as to … respond to [crisis] situations in areas surrounding Japan."

56. For a parallel with Europe, See Ian Manners, "Normative Power Europe: A Contradiction in Terms?," *Journal of Common Market Studies*, 40 (2),

2002, pp. 235–58, and Hans Maull, "Germany and Japan: The New Civilian Powers," *Foreign Affairs*, 69 (5), 1990, pp. 91–106.

57. Similarly, China's ambiguous position on Iran's nuclear programme is due in large measure to its energy needs. Beijing could invest up to USD 120 billion in the hydrocarbon sector in Iran (*New York Times*, 29 Sept. 2009).

4. CHINA, A GLOBAL POWER IN THE MAKING

1. On the semantic shift from "rise" to "development," see Benoît Vermander, *Chine brune ou Chine verte?*, p. 113.
2. See Goldman Sachs, "The N-11: More Than an Acronym," *Global Economics Paper*, 153, March 2007 (GDP and income per capita at market exchange rates). The effects of the crisis have further increased the differential in growth rates between China and the United States and accelerated the catching-up process.
3. Interview with Jim O'Neill, chief economist at Goldman Sachs, *Reuters*, 9 June 2009.
4. Forty-three per cent of China's population work on the land, producing 11 per cent of GDP. The corresponding figures for Japan are 4.4 and 1.4 per cent respectively.
5. EIU, *A New Ranking of the World's Most Innovative Countries*, 2009.
6. See "For an in-depth analysis of global patent portfolios," Corporate Invention Board, December 2009.
7. See OECD, *Science, Technology and Industry Outlook 2010*.
8. Its licence export/import ratio is thus 3.3, as against 2.2 for the United States and 1.6 for France.
9. See Thomson Reuters, *2008 Global Innovation Study*, 2009.
10. Japan Patent Office, "Japan's Technological Competitiveness from the Patent Viewpoint 2008," April 2009. The periods analysed are 2000–2006 for photovoltaic patents, 1995–2006 for vehicle patents.
11. This explains why Japanese pharmaceutical groups buy up foreign firms: in 2008 they acquired two American companies and an Indian firm at a total cost of USD 14 billion.
12. The discovery of carbon nanotubes is attributed to Sumio Iijima at NEC.
13. *Nikkei Weekly*, 20 October 2008. Another example is the space solar power system project, on which over 100 researchers have been working since 1998. The first station could be operational by 2030.
14. For a detailed description of these technologies, see Matsushita Electric Ltd., *Annual Report 2003*, p. 9.
15. METI, *White Paper on International Economy and Trade 2009*, Summary, p. 12.

16. Source: Ministry of Science and Technology of the PRC (MOST). Seven priority areas have been selected under the Plan, including microelectronics, aviation, aerospace and new materials.

17. Chinese press reports suggest that China could be able to send a man to the moon by 2020.

18. On China's innovation policy, see Shahid Yusuf and Kaoru Nabeshima, "Strengthening China's Technological Capability," *World Bank Policy Research Working Paper 4309*, 2007, and Martin Schaaper, "Measuring China's Innovation System," OECD, *STI Working Paper*, 2009/1.

19. Though the number of citations remains small.

20. China's Tianhe-1A system is already the world's fastest and most powerful supercomputer, according to the Top 500 ranking in November 2010, while the Nebulae/Dawning ranks third. Meanwhile, budget restrictions could cause Japan to freeze its own development programme.

21. *The Economist*, 23 April 2009.

22. Royalties paid abroad represent 20 per cent of the cost of each mobile phone made in China and 30 per cent of the cost of a computer (see *Chinanews*, 26 May 2006).

23. EIU, *A New Ranking*, pp. 8–9.

24. Samuel P. Huntington, *The Clash of Civilisations and the Remaking of the World Order*, New York: Simon & Schuster, 1996, p. 229.

25. John Mearsheimer, "Better to be Godzilla than Bambi," *Foreign Policy*, 146, Jan–Feb 2005.

26. On 13 October 2009, China protested strongly against Indian prime minister Manmohan Singh's visit to Arunachal Pradesh, regarded by Beijing as "South Tibet." On the relationship between China and India, see "China and India: Rivals Always, Partners Sometimes," Asia Centre, *China Analysis*, no. 24, August 2009.

27. See Jean-Pierre Cabestan and Benoît Vermander, *La Chine en quête de ses frontières. La confrontation Chine-Taiwan*, Paris: Presses de Sciences Po, 2005.

28. At a more practical level, China is a member of APEC and the ASEAN Regional Forum, groups for discussion about security in the Asia-Pacific region between Asian countries and Western powers.

29. India, Pakistan, Iran and Mongolia are observers.

30. See Russell Ong, *China's Security Interests in the 21st Century*, London: Routledge, 2007. The 1961 Security Treaty between China and North Korea is still in force; Russia terminated a similar treaty in 1992.

31. Between China, North and South Korea, the United States, Japan and Russia.

32. See Eric Teo Chu Cheo, "China, a Regional 'Soft Power'," *Politique étrangère*, 4, 2004.

33. On the concept of hegemonic stability, see Charles Kindleberger, *The World in Depression 1929–1939*, Berkeley: University of California Press, 1973.

34. See Christopher M. Dent (ed.), *China, Japan and Regional Leadership in East Asia*, Cheltenham: Edward Elgar, 2008, p. 159.

35. See Standard Bank, *BRIC and Africa*, 9 March 2011.

36. Oil accounts for 75 per cent of African exports to China, the second-largest market for African oil after the United States. See South African Institute of International Affairs, "China and Africa's Natural Resources," *Occasional Paper no. 41*, Sept. 2009.

37. Japan has also been quite active in this respect. In 1991, within the framework of the United Nations, it created the Tokyo International Conference on African Development (TICAD); in 2008, it promised to double official assistance and private investment by 2012 (TICAD IV), though this still represents only half the amount of Chinese aid.

38. See John Fox and François Godement, *A Power Audit of EU-China Relations*, Policy Report, European Council on Foreign Relations, 2009.

39. See USCC, *2010 Report to the Congress*, Nov. 2010, p. 19.

40. A term coined by Niall Ferguson, a Professor of History at Harvard University.

41. Worth USD 1,160 billion at end-March 2010, representing 13 per cent of total US Treasury securities and 25 per cent of the amount held outside the United States.

42. See Denny Roy, "China's Pitch for a Multipolar World: The New Security Concept," Asia-Pacific Center for Security Studies, 2(1), May 2003.

43. As could be seen at the Copenhagen climate summit, since China would regard supranational oversight of its energy and climate commitments as an infringement of its sovereignty.

44. US Department of Defense, *Annual Report to Congress. Military Power of the People's Republic of China 2007*, Washington DC, 2007, p. 6.

45. On the "peer competitor" concept, see Thomas Szanya et al., *The Emergence of Peer Competitors. A Framework for Analysis*, Santa Monica: Rand Corporation, 2001.

46. There has been escalation on the trade front since September 2009, with the US taxing steel tubes and tyres and China retaliating by raising tariffs on poultry and large cars.

47. In a success for China, G20 accepted its claim on 27 September 2009, to come into effect in 2011. Another success has been G20's replacement of G8 as the main forum for international consultation.

48. Sun Tzu, *The Art of War*, transl. Lionel Giles, Mineola: Dover Publications, 2002, Chapter 3.

49. See Joshua Cooper Ramo, *The Beijing Consensus*, London: Foreign Policy Centre, 2004. For a critique of the concept, see Andrew Leonard, "No consensus on the Beijing Consensus," Sept. 2006, http://www.salon.com/tech/htww/2006/09/15/beijing_consensus.

50. See Orion Lewis and Jessica Teets, "A China Model?," Glasshouse Forum, Sept. 2009, http://www.glasshouseforum.org.

51. John Mearsheimer, *The Tragedy of Great Power Politics*, New York: W.W. Norton, 2001, pp. 401–2.

52. US Department of Defense, *Annual Report to Congress. Military Power of the People's Republic of China 2010*, Washington DC, 2010, p. 43. The budget for 2011 shows an increase of 12.9 per cent to 601 billion yuan.

53. State Council of the People's Republic of China, *China's National Defense in 2006*, Beijing, Chapter 2.

54. China signed the 1968 Non-Proliferation Treaty in 1992, shortly after France. Until then, it had regarded the treaty as the hegemonic instrument of the American and Russian superpowers.

55. US Department of Defense, *Annual Report to Congress. Military Power of the People's Republic of China 2009*, Washington DC, 2009, p. 36.

56. *China Daily*, 16 April 2009.

57. US Department of Defense, *Annual Report to Congress. Military Power of the People's Republic of China 2009*, p. 58.

CONCLUSION

1. For example "Conceal a dagger in a smile" (*The 36 Stratagems*, 10th stratagem). The treatise, by an anonymous author, was probably written during the Ming dynasty (1368–1644).

2. At the same time, Ichiro Ozawa, the then "shadow shogun" and DPJ strongman, stepped up contacts with Beijing. In December 2009, he met president Hu Jintao during a mission he led as the head of a 640-strong delegation, including 143 DPJ MPs.

3. From a Japanese standpoint, the results on three major issues have been disappointing: the food safety of Chinese food exports, respect of intellectual property rights and extraction rights for gas fields in the China Sea.

4. Jean-Luc Domenach, *Comprendre la Chine d'aujourd'hui*, Paris: Perrin, 2007, p. 121.

5. Two-thirds of Japanese people have a poor opinion of China. In a Genron-NPO survey on 17 August 2007, almost 60 per cent of Chinese respondents thought that "militaristic" was the adjective that best described Japan.

6. According to Yukio Hatoyama, the creation of an East Asia Community would be the only way to overcome nationalism. See "My Political Philosophy," *Voice*.

7. On this subject, see Léon Vandemeersch, *Le nouveau monde sinisé*, Paris: PUF, 1986.
8. Tagore believed that Asia's spiritual contribution would regenerate a West sapped by materialism.
9. See Claude Meyer, "Hatoyama's Vision of an Asian Community—A European View," *Japan Spotlight*, Japan Economic Foundation, March 2010.
10. At the summit between Japan, Cambodia, Laos, Myanmar, Thailand and Vietnam on 7 November 2009, Japan promised USD 5.6 billion in official aid for the project in addition to the USD 4.5 billion committed since 2007.
11. See Goldman Sachs, *Global Economics Papers*, Nos. 99 and 153.
12. It currently represents half the world's population and 23.5 per cent of world GDP.
13. Contrary to the view put forward by Samuel Huntington in his well-known book, *The Clash of Civilisations*.
14. *People's Daily*, 21 May 2009.

BIBLIOGRAPHY

Acharya, A., *Regionalism and Multilateralism: Essays on Cooperative Security in the Asia Pacific*, Singapore: Eastern Universities Press, 2002.

Aglietta, M. and Landry, Y., *La Chine vers la superpuissance*, Paris: Economica, 2007.

Austin, G. and Harris, S., *Japan and Greater China—Political Economy and Military Power in the Asian Century*, London: Hurst & Co, 2001.

Bacani, C., *The China Investor: Getting Rich with the Next Superpower*, Indianapolis: John Wiley, 2003.

Bafoil, F., *What are we looking for by comparing EU and ASEAN?*, Paris: CERI, May 2009.

Bajpaee, C., "Chinese Energy Strategy in Latin America," *China Brief*, 5(14), June 2005.

Beeson, M., *Regionalism & Globalization in East Asia: Politics, Security and Economic Development*, Basingstoke: Palgrave Macmillan, 2007.

Bell, D., *China's New Confucianism*, Princeton: Princeton University Press, 2008.

Berger, T, "Set for stability? Prospects for conflict and cooperation in East Asia," *Review of International Studies*, 26, 2000, pp. 405–28.

Bergsten, F. and Ito, T., *No More Bashing: Building a New Japan-US Economic Relationship*, Washington DC: Institute for International Economics, 2001.

Bergsten, F., Gill, B., Lardy, N. and Mitchell, D., *China: What the World Needs to Know About the Emerging Superpower*, New York: Public Affairs, 2006.

Bergsten, F. et al., *China's Rise: Challenges and Opportunities*, Washington DC: Institute for International Economics, 2009.

Berkofsky, A., "China's Asian Ambitions," *Far Eastern Economic Review*, 168 (7), pp. 20–3, July–August 2005.

Bernstein, R. and Munro R., *The Coming Conflict with China*, New York: Vintage, 1998.

171

BIBLIOGRAPHY

Blank, S., "China's New Moves in the Central Asian Energy Sweepstakes," *China Brief*, 6 (3), February 2006.

Blecher, M., "Hegemony and Workers' Politics in China," *The China Quarterly*, 170, pp. 283–303, June 2002.

Bouissou, J-M. (dir.), *Le Japon contemporain*, Paris: Fayard/CERI, 2007.

—— *Quand les sumos apprennent à danser. La fin du modèle japonais*, Paris: Fayard, 2003.

Boyer, R. and Souyri, P., *Mondialisation et régulations. Europe et Japon face à la singularité américaine*, Paris: La Découverte, 2001.

Braunstein, E. and Epstein, G., "Bargaining power and foreign direct investment in China: Can 1.3 billion consumers tame the multinationals?," *Working Paper* no. 2002–13, New School University: Center for Economic Policy Analysis, 2002.

Bresciani, U., *Reinventing Confucianism. The New Confucian Movement*, Taipei: Taipei Ricci Institute, 2001.

Breslin, S., *China and the Global Political Economy*, Basingstoke: Palgrave Macmillan, 2007.

Cabestan, J-P. and Vermander, B., *La Chine en quête de ses frontières. La confrontation Chine-Taiwan*, Paris: Presses de Sciences Po, 2005.

Cabestan, J-P., "La montée en puissance de la diplomatie chinoise," in Boisseau du Rocher, S. (ed.), *Asie dix ans après la crise*, Paris: La Documentation française, 2007.

—— *La politique internationale de la Chine*, Paris: Presses de Sciences Po, 2010.

Cai, Y., "The Resistance of Chinese Laid-off Workers in the Reform Period," *The China Quarterly*, 170, pp. 327–44, June 2002.

Camilleri, J., *Regionalism in the New Asia-Pacific Order*, Cheltenham: Edward Elgar, 2003.

Chai, W., "The Ideological Paradigm Shifts of China's World View: From Marxism-Leninism-Maoism to the Pragmatism-Multilateralism of the Deng-Jiang-Hu Era," *Asian Affairs: an American Review*, 22 September 2003.

Chambers, M., "Framing the Problem: China's Threat Environment," *Asia Policy*, 4, pp. 61–6, July 2007.

Chan, G., Hu, W. and Zha, D., *China's International Relations in the 21st Century. Dynamics of Paradigm Shifts*, Lanham: University Press of America, 2000.

Chan, S., "Is There a Power Transition Between the U.S and China? The Different Faces of National Power," *Asian Survey* 15 (5), pp. 687–701, September–October 2005.

Chang, G., "Halfway to China's Collapse," *Far Eastern Economic Review*, 169 (5), pp. 25–8, June 2006.

BIBLIOGRAPHY

Chang, G., *The Coming Collapse of China*, New York: Random House, 2001.

Cheng, A., *Histoire de la pensée chinoise*, Paris: Seuil, coll. "Points," 2002.

Cheng, J., "The ASEAN-China Free Trade Area: Genesis and Implications," *Australian Journal of International Affairs*, 58(2), pp. 257–77, 2004.

Christensen, T., "Fostering Stability or Creating a Monster? The Rise of China and US Policy toward East Asia," *International Security*, 31(1), pp. 81–126, 2006.

Chung, J. H., "China and Northeast Asia: a Complex Equation for 'Peaceful Rise'," *Politics*, 27 (3), pp. 156–64, 2007.

Cornelius, P. and Story, J., "China Revolutionizes Energy Markets," *Far Eastern Economic Review*, 168 (9), pp. 21–4, October 2005.

Courmont, B., *Chine, la grande séduction*, Paris: Ed. Choiseul, 2009.

CRS Report to the Congress, *Social Unrest in China*, 2006.

Curtis, G., *The Logic of Japanese Politics: Leaders, Institutions and the Limits of Change*, New York: Columbia University Press, 1999.

——— (ed.), *Policymaking in Japan—Defining the Role of the Politicians*, Tokyo: JCIE, 2002.

Delamotte, G. and Godement, F. (eds.), *Géopolitique de l'Asie*, Paris: SEDES, 2007.

Delmas-Marty, M. and Will, P-E. (eds.), *La Chine et la Démocratie*, Paris: Fayard, 2007.

Deng, Y. and Moore, T., "China Views Globalization: Toward a New Great-Power Politics?," *The Washington Quarterly*, 27 (3), pp. 117–36, June 2004.

Dent, C., *China, Japan and Regional Leadership in East Asia*, Cheltenham: Edward Elgar, 2008.

Dent, C., *East Asian Regionalism*, London: Routledge, 2008.

Desker, B., "In Defence of FTAs: from Purity to Pragmatism in East Asia," *The Pacific Review*, 17 (1), pp. 3–26, 2004.

Domenach, J-L., *La Chine m'inquiète*, Paris: Perrin, 2008.

Dourille-Feer, E., Bouissou, J-M. and Yatabe, K., *Japon. Le renouveau?*, Paris: La Documentation française, 2002.

Downs, S., "The Chinese Energy Security Debate," *The China Quarterly*, pp. 21–41, March 2004.

Drifte, R., *Japan's Security Relations with China since 1989: From Balancing to Bandwagoning?*, London: Routledge, 2002.

Economy, E., *The River Runs Black. The Environmental Challenge to China's Future*, Ithaca: Cornell University Press, 2004.

Elvin, M., *The Retreat of the Elephants. An Environmental History of China*, New Haven: Yale University Press, 2004.

BIBLIOGRAPHY

Emmott, B., *The Sun Also Sets. Why Japan Will Not Be Number One*, London: Simon & Schuster, 1989.

—— *Rivals. How the Power Struggle Between China, India and Japan Will Shape Our Next Decade*, New York: Harcourt, 2008.

EU Chamber of Commerce in China, *Overcapacity in China*, November 2009

Felker, G., "Southeast Asian Industrialisation and the Changing Global Production System," *Third World Quarterly*, 24 (2), pp. 255–82, 2003.

Flouzat, D., *Japon, éternelle renaissance*, Paris: PUF, 2002.

Foot, R. "Chinese Strategies in a US-hegemonic Global Order: Accommodating and Hedging," *International Affairs*, 82 (1), 2006.

Fox, J. and Godement, F., *A Power Audit of EU-China Relations*, Policy Report, European Council on Foreign Relations, 2009.

Frankel, F. and Harding, H. (eds.), *The India-China Relationship. What the United States Need to Know*, New York: Columbia University Press, 2004.

Frankel, J., "New Estimation of China's Exchange Rate Regime," *NBER Working Paper*, 14700, February 2009.

Freeman, D., "Hu in Europe: Active Diplomacy amid Trade Friction," *China Brief*, 5 (24), November 2005.

Friedberg, A., "Ripe for Rivalry: Prospects for Peace in a Multipolar Asia," *International Security*, 18(3), pp. 5–33, 1993/4.

—— "The Struggle for Mastery in Asia," *Commentary*, 110 (4), pp. 17–26, 2000.

—— "The Future of US-China Relations: Is Conflict Inevitable?," *International Security*, Fall 2005.

Friedman, E., Pickowicz, P. and Selden, M., *Revolution, Resistance and Reform in Village China*, New Haven: Yale University Press, 2005.

Frost, E., *Asia's New Regionalism*, Boulder: Lynne Rienner, 2008.

Frost, S., "Chinese outward direct investment in Southeast Asia: how big are the flows and what does it mean for the region?," *The Pacific Review*, 17 (3), pp. 323–40, 2004.

Garver, J., *China and Iran. Ancient Partners in a Post-Imperial World*, Washington DC: University of Washington Press, 2006.

Gaulier, G., Lemoine, F. and Unal-Kesenci, D., "China's Integration in East Asia: Production Sharing, FDI and High-Tech Trade," *CEPII Working Paper*, no. 2005–09, June 2005.

—— "China's Emergence and the Reorganisation of Trade Flows in Asia," *CEPII Working Paper*, no. 2006–05, March 2006.

Gereffi, G. et al., "Getting the Numbers Right: International Engineering Education in the United States, China, and India," *Journal of Engineering Education*, 97 (1), January 2008.

Gill, B. and Huang, Y. "Sources and Limits of Chinese 'Soft Power'," *Survival*, Summer 2006.

BIBLIOGRAPHY

Gilley, B., "The Year China Started to Decline," *Far Eastern Economic Review*, 168 (8), pp. 32–5, September 2005.

Gipouloux, F., *La Méditerranée asiatique*, Paris: CNRS Editions, 2009.

Glosserman, B., "Fallout from Pyongyang: China's Prize," *Far Eastern Economic Review*, 168 (9), pp. 42–5, October 2005.

Gnesotto, N. and Grevi, G., "The New Global Puzzle. What World for the EU in 2025?," Institute for Security Studies, 2006.

Godement, F. (ed.), *China's Political Trends, Les Cahiers d'Asie*, no. 3, Paris: IFRI/Centre Asie, 2003.

Goldman Sachs, "Dreaming With BRICs: The Path to 2050," *Global Economics Paper*, 99, October 2003.

——— "The N-11: More Than an Acronym," *Global Economics Paper*, 153, March 2007.

Green, M. and Cronin, P., (eds.), *The US-Japan Alliance Past, Present and Future*, New York NY: Council on Foreign Relations Press, 1999.

Greg, A. and Stuart, H., *Japan and Greater China: Political Economy and Military Power in the Asian Century*, London: Hurst & Co., 2001.

Gries, P., *China's New Nationalism: Pride, Politics and Diplomacy*, Berkeley: University of California Press, 2004.

Haider, Z., "Oil Fuels Beijing's New Power Game," *Yale Global Online*, March 2005.

Harrison, S., *Japan's Nuclear Future—The Plutonium Debate and East-Asian Security*, Washington DC: Carnegie Endowment for International Peace, 1996.

Hatoyama, Y., "My Political Philosophy," *Voice*, September 2009.

Hauter, F., *Planète chinoise*, Paris: Carnets Nord, 2008.

He, J. and Kuijs, L., "Rebalancing China's Economy: Modelling a Policy Package," *World Bank Working Paper*, 7, September 2007.

Hempton-Jones, J., "The Evolution of China's Engagement with International Governmental Organizations. Toward a Liberal Foreign Policy?," *Asian Survey*, 15 (5), pp. 702–21, September–October 2005.

Hickey, D., *The Armies of East Asia: China, Taiwan, Japan, and the Koreas*, Boulder: Lynne Rienner, 2003.

Hilpert, H. and Haak, R., *Japan and China: Cooperation, Competition and Conflict*, Basingstoke: Palgrave Macmillan, 2002.

Hook, G. and Hasegawa, H. (eds.), *The Political Economy of Japanese Globalization*, London: Routledge, 2001.

Hook, L., "The Rise of China's New Left," *Far Eastern Economic Review*, 170 (3), pp. 8–14, April 2007.

Howe, C., *China and Japan: History, Trends and Prospects*, Oxford: Oxford University Press, 1996.

Huang, J., *Factionalism in Chinese Communist Politics*, Cambridge: Cambridge University Press, 2000.

Huang, Y., *Capitalism with Chinese Characteristics: Entrepreneurship and the State*, Cambridge: Cambridge University Press, 2008.

Hughes, C., *Japan's Re-emergence as a 'Normal' Military Power*, Oxford: Oxford University Press, 2004.

Huntington, S., *The Clash of Civilisations and The Remaking of the World Order*, New York: Simon & Schuster, 1996.

IMF, *Global Financial Stability Report*, April 2010 (updated July 2010).

———— *World Economic Outlook Report*, April 2010 (updated July 2010).

———— *Article IV Consultation with Japan*, July 2010.

Izraelewicz, E., *L'arrogance chinoise*, Paris: Grasset, 2011.

Japan Patent Office, "Japan's Technological Competitiveness from the Patent Viewpoint 2008," April 2009.

JETRO, *White Paper 2008*.

Jiang, W., "The Costs of China's Modernization," *China Brief*, 5 (25), December 2005.

———— "The Dragon's Thirst for Canadian Oil," *China Brief*, 5 (11), May 2005.

Johnson, A. and Ross, R. (eds.), *New Directions in the Studies of China's Foreign Policy*, Stanford: Stanford University Press, 2006.

Johnson, C., *Japan: Who Governs? The Rise of the Developmental State*, New York: Norton, 1995.

Katz, R., *Japanese Phoenix: The Long Road to Economic Revival*, Armonk: ME Sharpe, 2003.

Katzenstein, P., "Japan in the American Imperium: Rethinking Security," *The Asia-Pacific Journal—Japan Focus*, October 2008.

Katzenstein, P., *Rethinking Japanese Security*, London: Routledge, 2008.

Katzenstein, P. and Shiraishi, T. (eds.), *Beyond Japan: East Asian Regionalism*, Ithaca: Cornell University Press, 2006.

Katzenstein, P., *A World of Regions: Asia and Europe in the American Imperium*, Ithaca and London: Cornell University Press, 2005.

Keller, W. and Rawski, T. (eds.), *China's Rise and the Balance of Influence in Asia*, Pittsburgh: University of Pittsburgh Press, 2007.

Kennedy P., *The Rise and Fall of the Great Powers*, New York: Vintage Books, 1989.

Kornai, J., "What the Change of System from Socialism to Capitalism Does and Does Not Mean," *Journal of Economic Perspectives*, 14 (1), pp. 27–42, Winter 2000.

Kuik, C-C., "Multilateralism in China's Asean Policy: Its Evolution, Characteristics, and Aspiration," *Contemporary Southeast Asia*, 27 (1), pp. 102–22, 2005.

BIBLIOGRAPHY

Lam, W., "SARS: Growing Impact on China's Leadership," *China Brief*, 3 (9), May 2003.

Lampton, D. (ed.), *The Making of Chinese Foreign Policy and Security Policy in the Era of Reform, 1978–2000*, Stanford: Stanford University Press, 2001.

—— *Same Bed, Different Dreams. Managing U.S.-China Relations, 1989–2000*, Berkeley: University of California Press, 2001.

Lardy, N., *Integrating China in the Global Economy*, Washington DC: The Brookings Institution Press, 2002.

Lemoine, F. and Unal-Kesenci, D., "China in the International Segmentation of Production Processes," *CEPII Working Paper*, no. 2002–02, 2002.

Lemoine, F., *L'économie chinoise*, Paris: La Découverte, 2006.

Leonard, A., "No Consensus on the Beijing Consensus," September 2006. http://www.salon.com/technology/how_the_world_works/2006/09/15/beijing_consensus

Leonard, F., *Que pense la Chine?*, Paris: Plon, 2008.

Lewis, O. and Teets, J., "A China Model?," Glasshouse Forum, September 2009.

Li, R., *A Rising China and Security in East Asia: Identity Construction and Security Discourse*, London: Routledge, 2008.

Lieberthal, K. and Oksenberg, M., *Policy Making in China: Leaders, Structures, and Processes*, Princeton: Princeton University Press, 1988.

Lin, J., "Changing China's Growth Model," *Far Eastern Economic Review*, 168 (9), pp. 52–3, October 2005.

Liu, B. and Piachaud, D., "Urbanization and Social Policy in China," *Asia-Pacific Development Journal*, 13 (1), pp. 1–26, June 2006.

Maddison, A., *Chinese Economic Performance in the Long Run: 960–2030 AD*, Paris: OECD, 2007.

—— *The World Economy: A Millennial Perspective*, Paris: OECD, 2001.

Mahbubani, K., "Understanding China," *Foreign Affairs*, September 2005.

Manners, I., "Normative Power Europe: A Contradiction in Terms?," *Journal of Common Market Studies*, 40 (2), pp. 235–58, 2002

Mao, Y., "Beijing's Two-Pronged Iraq Policy," *China Brief*, 5 (12), May 2005.

Maull, H., "Germany and Japan: The New Civilian Powers," *Foreign Affairs*, 69 (5), pp. 91–106, 1990.

McGray, D., "Japan's Gross National Cool," *Foreign Policy*, May 2002.

McKinsey., "Global Investment Strategies for China's Financial Institutions," *McKinsey Quarterly*, June 2008.

—— "Private Ownership: The Real Source of China's Economic Miracle," *McKinsey Quarterly*, December 2008.

Mearsheimer, J., *The Tragedy of Great Power Politics*, New York: Norton, 2001.

BIBLIOGRAPHY

Mengin, F. and Rocca, J. L. (eds.), *Politics in China. Moving Frontiers*, New York: Palgrave, 2002

METI, *Summary of the 37th Survey on Overseas Business Activities*, 2008.

——— *White Paper on International Economy and Trade*, 2009.

Meyer, C., "PM Hatoyama's Vision of an Asian Community—A European View," *Japan Spotlight*, Japan Economic Foundation, March 2010.

——— "Should China Revalue its Currency? Lessons from the Japanese Experience," GEM-Sciences Po, Policy Brief, April 2008.

——— "Le face-à-face Chine/Japon," *Etudes*, December 2006.

——— "Le tournant des années 1980. L'économie à l'épreuve de la mondialisation: deux défis, deux ambitions," in Bouissou, J-M. (ed.), *Le Japon contemporain*, Paris: Fayard, 2007.

——— "L'énigme japonaise," *Etudes*, May 2002.

——— "Les relations Inde-Japon: vers un partenariat global?" in Racine, J-L. (ed.), *L'Inde et l'Asie. Nouveaux équilibres, nouvel ordre mondial*, Paris: CNRS Editions, 2009.

——— *La Puissance financière du Japon*, pref. Christian Sautter, Paris: Economica, 1996.

Miller, L., "In Search of China's Energy Authority," *Far Eastern Economic Review*, 169 (1), January–February 2006.

Missions économiques en Chine, *S'implanter en Chine 2009*, Paris: Ubifrance, 2009.

Morris, L-M., *Japon. L'essentiel d'un marché*, Paris: Ubifrance, 2009.

Mulgan, A., *Japan's Failed Revolution: Koizumi and the Politics of Economic Reform*, Sydney: Asia Pacific Press, 2002

Naughton, B., *The Chinese Economy: Transitions and Growth*, Cambridge: MIT Press, 2007.

Nenkivell, N., "China's Pollution and its Threat to Domestic and Regional Stability," *China Brief*, 5 (22), October 2005.

Niquet, V., *Chine-Japon, l'affrontement*, Paris: Perrin, 2006.

Norberg, J., "China Paranoia Derails Free Trade," *Far Eastern Economic Review*, 169 (1), January–February 2006.

Nye, J., *Soft Power: The Means To Success In World Politics*, New York: Public Affairs, 2004

Oberhaitmann, A., "Le secteur de l'énergie et la protection de l'environnement en Chine," *Perspectives chinoises*, 69, pp. 39–52, January–February 2002.

Odgaard, L. and Biscop, S., "The EU and China: Partners in Effective Multilateralism?," in Kerr, D. and Fei, L. (eds.), *The International Politics of EU-China Relations*, Oxford: Oxford University Press, 2007.

OECD, *Economic Survey: China*, Paris, 2005.

——— *Economic Survey: China*, Paris, 2010.

——— *China in the World Economy*, Paris, 2002.

BIBLIOGRAPHY

———— *Economic Survey: Japan*, Paris, 2009.

Ong, R., *China's Security Interests in the 21st Century*, London: Routledge, 2007

Park, J., "How China can bring Sunshine to Korea," *Far Eastern Economic Review*, 169 (5), pp. 29–31, June 2006.

———— "Inside Multilateralism: The Six-Party Talks," *The Washington Quarterly*, 28 (4), pp. 75–91, Autumn 2005.

Patrick, H., "Japan's Deep Recession and Prolonged Recovery," Center on Japanese Economy and Business: Columbia Business School, September 2009.

Patrick, H. et al., *Reviving Japan's Economy: Problems and Prescriptions*, Cambridge: MIT Press, 2005.

Planel, N., *Un autre Japon (2001–2006)*, Paris: Mille et une nuits, 2007.

Poupée, K., *Les Japonais*, Paris: Taillandier, 2008.

Ramo, J., *The Beijing Consensus*, London: Foreign Policy Centre, 2004.

Roy, D., "China's Pitch for a Multipolar World: The New Security Concept," *Asia-Pacific Center for Security Studies*, 2 (1), May 2003.

Sabouret, J-F. (ed.), *L'Empire de l'intelligence. Politiques scientifiques et technologiques du Japon depuis 1945*, Paris: CNRS Editions, 2007.

Sako, M., *Shifting Boundaries of the Firm: Japanese Company—Japanese Labor*, Oxford: Oxford University Press, 2006.

Samuels, R., *Securing Japan. Tokyo's Grand Strategy and the Future of East Asia*, New York: Cornell University Press, 2007.

Sanjuan, T. (ed.), *Dictionnaire de la Chine contemporaine*, Paris: Armand Colin, 2007.

Schaaper, M., "Measuring China's Innovation System," OECD, *STI Working Paper*, 2009/1.

Seizelet, E. and Serra, R., *Le pacifisme à l'épreuve. Le Japon et son armée*, Paris: Les Belles Lettres, 2009.

Shambaugh, D., "China's Propaganda System Institutions, Processes and Efficacy," *The China Journal*, 57, pp. 27–58, January 2007.

———— "The New Strategic Triangle: US and European Reactions to China's Rise," *The Washington Quarterly*, 28 (3), Summer 2005

———— *Modernizing China's Military. Progress, Problems and Prospects*, Berkeley: University of California Press, 2002.

———— (ed.), *Power Shift: China's and Asia's New Dynamics*, Berkeley: University of California Press, 2005.

Shichor, Y., "Sudan: China's Outpost in Africa," *China Brief*, 5 (21), October 2005.

Shirk, S., *China, Fragile Superpower*, Oxford: Oxford University Press, 2007.

Short, P., *Mao: A Life*, London: John Murray, 2004

Soderberg, M. (ed.), *Chinese-Japanese Relations in the Twenty-First Century: Complementarity and Conflict*, London: Routledge, 2002.

BIBLIOGRAPHY

Spence, J., *The Search for Modern China*, New York: Norton, 1991.

Stalley, P. and Yang D., "An Emerging Environmental Movement in China?," *The China Quarterly*, pp. 333–56, June 2006.

State Council of the People's Republic of China, *China's National Defense in 2006*, Beijing, 2007.

——— *Environmental Protection in China*, Beijing, June 2006.

Stiglitz, J., *Towards a New Model of Development. Remarks Prepared for the China Development Forum*, Beijing, March 2007.

Sudo, S., *The International Relations of Japan and South East Asia: Forging a New Regionalism*, London: Routledge, 2002.

Szayna, T. et al., *The Emergence of Peer Competitors. A Framework for Analysis*, Santa Monica: Rand Corporation, 2001.

Tailor, I., "Beijing's Arms and Oil Interests in Africa," *China Brief*, 5 (21), October 2005.

Teo Chu Cheow, E., "Asian Reactions to the Avian Flu Crisis: Lessons for Beijing," *China Brief*, 4 (5), March 2004.

——— "China at the Center of Asian Economic Integration," *China Brief*, 4 (15), July 2004.

Terrill, R., *The New Chinese Empire and What It Means for the United States*, New York: Basic Books, 2003.

Tertrais, B., "Problématiques stratégiques en Asie à l'horizon 2025: essai de prospective," *Recherches & Documents*, 12, Fondation pour la Recherche Stratégique, November 2008.

Thompson, D., "Beijing's Participation in UN Peacekeeping Operations," *China Brief*, 5 (11), May 2005.

Tow, W. et al., *Asia-Pacific Security. US, Australia and Japan and the New Security Triangle*, London: Routledge, 2008.

Tucker, N. (ed.), *Dangerous Strait. The US-Taiwan-China Crisis*. New York: Columbia University Press, 2005.

Unger, J. (ed.), *The Nature of Chinese Politics*, Armonk: ME Sharpe, 2002.

US Department of Defense, *Annual Report to Congress. Military Power of the People's Republic of China 2009*, Washington DC, 2009.

Vermander, B., *Chine brune ou Chine verte? Les dilemmes de l'Etat-parti*, Paris: Presses de Sciences Po, 2007.

Wang, H., "Multilateralism in Chinese Foreign Policy. The Limits of Socialization," *Asian Survey*, 40 (3), May–June 2000.

Wang, J., "China's Search for Stability with America," *Foreign Affairs*, September–October 2005.

Wei, S., Wen, J. and Zhou, H. (eds.), *The Globalization of the Chinese Economy*, Cheltenham: Edward Elgar, 2002.

Wei, Y., "Rural-Urban Migrant Workers in China: The Vulnerable Group in Cities," 2006.

BIBLIOGRAPHY

Weston, T. and Jensen, L. (eds.), *China Beyond the Headlines*, Lanham: Rowman & Littlefield, January 2000.

Wilson, D. and Purushothaman, R., "Dreaming With BRICs: The Path to 2050," Goldman Sachs, *Global Economics Paper*, 99, 2003.

Wood, C., *The Bubble Economy—The Japanese Economic Collapse*, Tokyo: Charles E. Tuttle, 1992.

World Bank & SEPA, *The Cost of Pollution in China*, 2007.

——— *An East Asian Renaissance*, 2007.

——— *China 2020: Development Challenges in the New Century*, Washington DC, 1997.

——— *The East Asian Miracle*, New York: Oxford University Press, 1993.

Wu, F., "Urban Poverty and Marginalization under Market Transition: The Case of Chinese Cities," *International Journal of Urban and Regional Research*, 28 (2), pp. 401–23, June 2004.

Yang, G., "How Do Chinese Civic Associations Respond to the Internet? Findings from a Survey," *China Quarterly*, 189, pp. 122–43, March 2007.

Yee, H. and Storey, I., *The China Threat: Perceptions, Myths and Reality*, London: Routledge, 2002.

You, J., "Why Are the Six-Party Talks Failing? A Chinese Perspective," *China Brief*, 5 (9), April 2005.

Yuan, J., "China and the Iranian Nuclear Crisis," *China Brief*, 6 (3), February 2006.

——— "China's Conditional Multilateralism and Great Power Entente," Strategic Studies Institute, January 2000.

Yusuf, S. and Nabeshima, K., "Strengthening China's Technological Capability," *World Bank Policy Research Working Paper*, 4309, 2007.

Zha, D., "An Opening for US-China Cooperation," *Far Eastern Economic Review*, 169 (5), pp. 44–7, May 2006.

Zhang, M. and Montaperto, R., *A Triad of Another Kind: The United States, China, and Japan*, Basingstoke: Macmillan, 1999.

Zhao, S. (ed.), *Chinese Foreign Policy. Pragmatism and Strategic Behavior*, Armonk: ME Sharpe, 2004.

——— *A Nation-State in Construction. Dynamics of Modern Chinese Nationalism*, Stanford: Stanford University Press, 2004.

——— *Prisoner of the State*, New York: Simon & Schuster, 2009.

Zheng, B., "China's 'Peaceful Rise' to Great-Power Status," *Foreign Affairs*, September–October 2005.

Zou, W., "The Changing Face of Rural Enterprises," *China Perspectives*, 50, November–December 2003.

Zweig, D., *Internationalizing China: Domestic Interest and Global Linkages*, Ithaca NY: Cornell University Press, 2002.

INDEX

INDEX

INDEX

INDEX